MEDIA POWER

HOW YOUR BUSINESS CAN PROFIT FROM THE MEDIA

Peter G. Miller

Dearborn
Financial Publishing, Inc.

Dedication
To Herman Albert Miller

While a great deal of care has been taken to provide accurate and current information, the ideas, suggestions, general principles and conclusions presented in this book are subject to local, state and federal laws and regulations, court cases and any revisions of same. The reader is thus urged to consult legal counsel regarding any points of law—this publication should not be used as a substitute for competent legal advice.

Publisher: Kathleen A. Welton
Associate Editor: Karen A. Christensen
Senior Project Editor: Jack L. Kiburz
Interior Design: Lucy Jenkins
Cover Design: Sam Concialdi

©1991 by Peter G. Miller

Published by Dearborn Financial Publishing, Inc.

Printed in the United States of America

91 92 93 10 9 8 7 6 5 4 3 2 1

Library of Congress Cataloging-in-Publication Data

Miller, Peter G.
    Media power : how your business can profit from the media / Peter G. Miller.
        p.   cm.
    Includes index.
    ISBN 0-79310-269-3
    1. Industrial publicity—United States.   2. Marketing—United States—Management.   3. Mass media and business—United States.
I. Title.
HD59.6.U6M55   1991
659—dc20   91-17967
                                                                          CIP

C O N T E N T S

P R E F A C E

Few industries are more visible yet less understood than the media. We constantly see what someone, somewhere has defined as "newsworthy," but how such decisions are made is largely a mystery. And since the process of turning data into news is so unclear, it's tough to get coverage because most of us don't know who to call or what to say.

As someone with experience as a reporter, writer and broadcaster, and as someone with experience as a promoter, I've seen both sides of the news gathering process. The system is rational, it does make sense and most people can earn coverage once they understand how it works.

This book is designed to serve as a promoter's introduction to the media, to show what journalists want and need and to explain how professionals can obtain ongoing news coverage that will lead to additional sales, profits and prestige. No less important, the strategies that work so well with the media can also enhance communication with clients and customers.

Peter G. Miller

Silver Spring, Maryland
January, 1991

ACKNOWLEDGMENTS

This book is based on my experiences and observations gained over 20 years as well as text that has been carefully written, rewritten and refined for this publication.

Originally developed as a series of weekly columns for the *Washington Business Journal*, the base material was later revised and expanded to create a book entitled *Media Marketing*. Portions of that book, in turn, were reprinted in the *Public Relations Quarterly* (Summer, 1989) and the *Public Relations Directory* for the metropolitan Washington area (Fall, 1989).

The current guide has been refined to deal directly with the needs of professionals and business executives. Core advice and concepts have been supplemented with examples and programs for a professional readership.

The author would like to thank Kathleen A. Welton and Karen A. Christensen, respectively my publisher and editor with Dearborn Financial Publishing, for their advice, ideas and support. Their assistance in this project has been greatly valued.

Also, readers should note that the quotation on page 3 is from John Naisbitt's *Megatrends*, Warner Books, Inc., Copyright 1982, 1984 by John Naisbitt. Used with permission.

Information concerning the Charles Cudd Company, page 13, was provided by *The Housing Executive Report* (P.O. Box 911, Millsboro, DE 19966) and is used with permission.

Material from an article by the author entitled "Be Your Own Publicist" has been incorporated within this book. The article was published December, 1990, by *Home Office Computing* (730 Broadway, New York, NY 10003). Copyright 1990 Scholastic Inc. Used with permission.

Except for Tylenol brand products, the Charles Cudd Company and the Blue Crab Bay Co., individual and organizational names used in examples throughout this book are entirely fictitious. Any resemblance between the examples used in this text and actual persons, living or dead, or actual organizations, past or present, or actual places or events is entirely coincidental.

Endorsements associated with this book reflect individual views only. Organizational names and titles are listed for informational purposes and do not imply or infer an organizational endorsement, recommendation or evaluation.

How To Contact the Author

Mr. Miller provides consulting services for selected businesses, associations and non-profit organizations nationwide. Requests for information concerning such services, as well as inquiries about the availability of the author for speeches and seminars, may be directed to Mr. Miller at the address below.

Readers of this guide are also welcome to contact the author with comments and ideas for future editions.

Peter G. Miller
Springhill Media Center
14 Saddlerock Court
Silver Spring, MD 20902

CHAPTER

1

Why Media Marketing?

Few institutions are more ingrained in our daily lives than the media. We awake to the radio and read the morning paper. By day we scan magazines, newspapers and newsletters and by night we tune in the evening news and read books. There's no doubt that much of our time is devoted to absorbing and reacting to what we read, see and hear.

But for many of us, it's not enough to just receive information. We want more from the media and by *more*, we mean access. We want to appear in print and on the air. We want to promote our ideas, publicize our products and enhance our names. We want access for reasons of commerce and ego, because appearing in the media creates a certain cachet, importance, currency and credibility machines can't build and dollars can't buy.

Yet as much as we want media access, most of our efforts to reach print and broadcast outlets fail. An informal survey of one Washington news bureau showed that it received nearly 2,000 news releases, announcements and letters, plus more than 100 telephone contacts—in a single week! Of all these pleas, pitches and petitions, not more than 1 or 2 percent ever found their way into print.

The story in newsrooms around the country is basically the same. Substantial amounts of time and money are spent developing campaigns that often produce few tangible results. Visit any news operation, whether it's print or broadcast, and you're certain to find piles of discarded news releases, unused photos and unread documents. Judging from the large number of promotional efforts that fail, it's clear few people understand how journalists work or why they choose one story and not another.

But while promotional failures are common, some professionals, businesses and individuals are successful and receive positive coverage on a continuing basis.

How do they do it?

All promoters are different and the precise strategy that works for one may not work for another. Yet despite differences, successful promoters do have something in common: They behave within definable guidelines that can be observed, measured and copied by others.

This is a book about the media; how information is obtained, packaged and distributed; how you can obtain ongoing news coverage; and the sales, profits and prestige that flow from such attention. Based on training, experience and observation over a period of more than 20 years, it argues that media access is not reserved for corporate giants or presidential candidates. You're important and reporters would like to hear from you, *but only if you know how the system works and how to package your ideas.* In turn, if more people are familiar with the news business, journalists will spend less time sorting through unusable news releases and unworkable story proposals.

COMPETING IN THE INFORMATION AGE

Understanding how the media works is not merely a matter of idle curiosity. Whether you're a real estate broker or a banker, an insurance agent or an attorney, having access to the media on a continuing, positive and productive basis is a decided advantage, one that often can be measured in terms of enhanced prestige, greater recognition and larger revenues.

An understanding of the media is not only important today, but it is probable that such information will become increasingly important in the coming years. The reason: Our growing development as an information-based society.

In his best-selling book, *Megatrends*, John Naisbitt demonstrates how we have moved from an industrial society to an information society where the majority of our people, some 65 percent according to Naisbitt, "create, process and distribute" information. In addition, Naisbitt makes this point:

> In an industrial society, the strategic resource is capital; a hundred years ago, a lot of people may have known how to build a steel plant, but not very many could get the money to build one. Consequently, access to the system was limited. But in our new society, as Daniel Bell first pointed out, the *strategic* resource is information. Not the only resource, but the most important. With information as the strategic resource, access to the economic system is much easier. (emphasis his)

If it's true that information is our new capital and we now have an information society, it's also true that information per se is not particularly valuable in isolation. A cure for cancer would be wonderful, but if the discovery is made by a hermit who refuses to share his secret, few if any people will benefit.

To have maximum value, information must be widely disbursed, freely received, evaluated and then redistributed so the entire cycle can begin again. For this process to be successful, to avoid the problem of ideas in isolation, there must be lines of communication and those lines are what we call the media. Specialized magazines, business weeklies, cable TV, books, phone calls, company newsletters, morning newspapers, computer networks, letters to clients, radio broadcasts and direct-mail campaigns are all examples of the media.

MEDIA MARKETING DEFINED

With so many media outlets available, and with so much demand by those outlets for stories and ideas, there must be a reasonable process to obtain coverage on a consistent basis.

What Is the Fourth Estate?

Journalists are often described as members of the "fourth estate," a description that raises the question, What is the fourth estate?

In Europe during the Middle Ages it was felt that there were three estates or classes—the nobility, the clergy and the common people. The press didn't really fit into any of the existing classes and so in the 1800s the term *fourth estate* came into use as a shorthand expression for journalists.

Today, government has replaced the nobility and the press has become the media. Still, the concept of the fourth estate applies: The media is separate and apart from the rest of us.

There is such a process, a body of principles, concepts and approaches we'll call media marketing. Media marketing can be defined as strategies and actions designed to promote products, persons, events, ideas and organizations through positive media attention year after year.

The expression *media marketing* is probably less familiar than the term *public relations*, but media marketing seems more appropriate for several reasons.

Within the field of public relations are many people who are perfectly capable of packaging ideas to attract media attention. Indeed, some individuals within the public relations field have extensive media backgrounds and could just as easily vie for jobs in journalism as in promotion if they so elected.

The term *public relations* carries excess baggage that makes it less appealing or precise than media marketing. Yes, there are knowledgeable professionals in public relations, but public relations is not a defined field such as real estate brokerage, law or medicine.

To practice brokerage, law or medicine, or to be a plumber, accountant, barber, embalmer or whatever, you need a license. And by having a licensure requirement there is a presumption of training, experience and a basic standard of performance.

Media versus Medium

What do we call newspapers, TV and radio? They are the media when grouped collectively, as in "media reports say the war is going well."

In formal language, a single newspaper might be called a medium, but the term is convoluted and most people will not use it. No one says, "I read the medium this morning and rain is expected tomorrow."

For our purposes, *media* is a collective term that describes more than one communication outlet or mode of contact, while a *medium* is someone who purports to see the future.

In public relations (and in journalism) there are no licensure laws, a situation that has its positive points. Unnecessary degrees, irrelevant tests and the general problem of excess "credentialism" are avoided. Anyone can enter the field, including people who champion unpopular and unorthodox ideas.

Having no licensure rules also means something else: Anyone can claim to be "in public relations" and as a consequence the expression is used widely.

Not only might someone "in public relations" be a communications or marketing expert, he or she may also be— judging from various classified advertisements— a telephone solicitor, receptionist or an individual with an attractive personality and a driver's license.

The public relations professionals in whom we are most interested obviously do not act as telephone solicitors or receptionists. They have a sizable array of skills and expertise and, to describe more precisely their interests and activities, it makes sense to use a more specific term than public relations. "Media marketing" comes closest to describing the areas that interest us most: understanding how the media works and how ideas can be packaged for maximum exposure.

Media marketing could be used literally by those who sell newspapers or TV stations. One could imagine a media broker—someone who sells newspapers or radio stations—

PR and the Big Business Connection

In the early 1900s big business was the subject of scathing articles and books by such muckrakers as Upton Sinclair and Ida Tarbell. There were few industry spokesmen to respond, a gap soon filled by business writers who saw that they could earn more as publicity agents than as journalists.

Publicity agents, the forerunners of today's more sophisticated public relations practitioners, became common not only in industry, but also with unions, associations and government. While publicity agents did much to open up the organizations they served, not everyone was pleased by their efforts to influence press coverage. The government, for its part, was so distressed by the new practice of public relations that in 1913 it prohibited the hiring of publicity agents. To this day the government has vast armies of information officers but not a single public relations practitioner.

---

saying that he or she is in media marketing, but for most people the term works nicely to characterize the interests of this book and those who read it.

There is another reason the term *public relations* seems inappropriate. It's ironic that the very expression *public relations* often has a negative connotation. We hear and read about "PR stunts" or that the position of a political candidate is "just public relations." Egomaniacs are said to "believe their own PR."

These expressions devalue an important concept. *People and organizations have an innate right to present themselves as best they can and to appear in the media as frequently as they can generate interest.* There's nothing wrong, unfair or unethical about self-interest. Newspapers, magazines and broadcast outlets all have active public relations departments because they recognize that media marketing is a valuable tool in the ongoing race for more distinction, greater circulation, higher ratings and ultimately a better bottom line.

THE IMPORTANCE OF MEDIA ACCESS

If we are now in an information society, if Naisbitt, Bell and others are right, then access to the media—the crucial network through which we all communicate—is critically important.

Think about it this way. In the coming year, several hundred thousand people will become licensed as real estate agents, the number of insurance brokers will proliferate and banking will become far more competitive. We'll continue to churn out CPAs and financial planners at a rapid rate and another 30,000 or 40,000 law students will graduate.

The number of competitors in virtually every business and profession is increasing, but while we have more people vying for clients and customers we do not necessarily have more business to divide. We have reached a point where many fields are saturated with well-trained, highly qualified professionals, and the result is a buyer's market of sorts, an environment where the number of those who buy services is insufficient to support the growing army of professionals who covet their business.

What has happened in dentistry may well occur in other fields. A flood of dental graduates coupled with a decline in tooth decay has created a gross surplus of dentists. Traditional drill-and-fill practices are no longer assured money-makers and as a result many dentists have left the field or turned to such specialties as cosmetic dentistry to pay the rent.

Today it is not enough to have credentials and a quality product. Image and perception often spell the difference between success and failure in many fields, and the practical reality is that those who communicate best have a stunning advantage over would-be competitors. Here's why.

First, promotional skills are essential in many fields where products and services are often indistinguishable.

In the eternal search for market distinction, individuals and businesses try to stand out in the midst of competitive clutter. Because a large number of substantially similar choices are available in most fields, it's difficult for consumers, users, buyers or clients to objectively select one competitor and not another. Since the alternatives are basically alike, there are no wrong choices and therefore *decisions are often made on the basis of familiarity and name recognition, major by-products of media attention.*

If we need insurance and the cost of one whole life policy is much like another, which policy do we choose? All brokers will tell us they have the best deal, yet surely such policies seem largely identical.

In many fields, product distinctions are unclear and one result is that we're encouraged to have brand loyalty, not because we particularly benefit, but because brand names are often the only way the products of one firm can be distinguished from those of another.

Blindfold 100 people, have them ride in cars of similar size and cost, and the probability of any of them matching an auto's comforts and ride with specific brand names is just about zero. The story is much the same with adhesive bandages, writing paper, photocopies, washing machines, paper tissues, gasoline, eyeglass lenses, canned corn and tires, to cite a few examples. Indeed, it's entirely common for one factory to produce identical products, which are then marketed under different, and sometimes competing, labels.

The world of services is even more perplexing. Professions have a way of homogenizing their practitioners. The person who finishes at the top of his or her class in medical school and the individual with the lowest passing grades are both known by the same title after graduation: Doctor. For the public, it's tough to tell who's best, who's the most competent or why one should be selected over another.

If there are 100 lawyers in town and you need a will, which attorney do you choose? They all went to law school. They all graduated and passed a standardized bar exam. So who do you select? The one nearby? The one with the fanciest furniture—and perhaps the highest fee? The one your neighbor used?

As hard as it may be for service users to make distinctions among service providers, it's also difficult for providers themselves to demonstrate differences. In the modern sense, there is little marketing experience in many fields, in part because until recently licensure laws often banned advertising as undignified or unprofessional. Now that marketing is increasingly widespread in every field and profession, prices in many specialties have declined, but to a surprising degree at least one old problem remains: How do you find the best lawyer, broker, banker, doctor or dentist?

We've replaced one form of clutter with another. Before, it was hard to choose professionals because there were few objective standards by which they could be judged. Now it's hard to judge professionals because advertising tells us not who is best, but who is available.

Given few objective clues, a consumer may well opt to buy from the car manufacturer who wins the most races and gets the most name recognition, rather than the firm that quietly concentrates on building a better vehicle. The broker quoted in the real estate pages will receive more referrals than the broker who makes little effort to market his or her services. The attorney who writes a weekly legal affairs column will stand out, not necessarily because he or she is—or is not—the world's leading legal authority in a given specialty, but because his or her name is familiar.

Second, we increasingly define importance by the extent of media coverage received. If it's not in the media, it isn't important. Conversely, receiving media coverage creates importance.

Suppose we have two candidates for political office. Barringer is athletic, telegenic, speaks well and has faithfully memorized 26 position papers prepared by his advisers. Springer, his primary opponent, is 90 pounds overweight, wears suits long out of style and has an entire campaign based on two fliers typed at home.

Who gets the most attention? Barringer. Why? Because he's a media-oriented candidate. His ideas on a variety of subjects, or at least his adviser's ideas, have been carefully prepared and written out. Every night a TV station features a 20-second sound bite from one of his stump speeches. Barringer is seen as the "stronger" candidate because he gets more exposure, and, in circular fashion, because he gets more exposure he *is* the stronger candidate. If Springer ever won, his victory would be described as a "major upset," not because he beat a candidate who was better, but because he defeated someone with greater media access.

Third, to gain media attention, size and money are important, but not as important as creativity and packaging.

Media marketing is among the most democratic activities we have. Anyone can play; you don't need a huge inheritance or a powerful job to gain press attention (though such assets may help).

Journalists want story concepts that interest their readers, viewers and listeners. If you've got such an idea and you know how to package it, the probability of getting coverage is excellent. If you haven't got a workable idea, then money, power and position are worth little. Wastepaper baskets in newsrooms across the country are filled with releases from the nation's largest firms and most prestigious institutions, organizations that—despite their size and dollars—failed to understand the media's essential needs.

Some may read these words and argue that while promotion is important, you don't need journalists to appear in print or on the air. Why bother with media marketing when you can buy as much space and time as you want, or at least as much as you can afford? The answer, as we shall now explain, is that advertising and editorial coverage involve markedly different values.

ADS VERSUS MEDIA MARKETING

Media access is most often seen in terms of advertising. If you want to reach a particular audience, the easiest and most direct approach is to buy space or time in the media of your choice.

Advertising is a multi-billion-dollar industry, and it's hard to believe a business of such size is possible without an observable record of success. Certainly, advertising does offer benefits; each year selected products and services increase sales and expand their market share because of successful ad campaigns.

Yet the concept of advertising is not always attractive or plausible. It presumes, by definition, that would-be advertisers have money to spend, an unlikely situation for new firms, companies operating at a loss or organizations with limited revenues.

Even if you have the money, advertising still poses several challenges: Audiences must be defined, themes and concepts developed and the entire presentation packaged creatively.

Given these requirements, developing productive ads isn't simple and results are not guaranteed.

Ads also must be placed with great care. Ads compete not only among themselves for the time and attention of readers, viewers and listeners, but they also compete with the editorial material they surround.

If you're an advertiser, you want your ad to appear in a successful medium that attracts a specific audience, yet you don't want a medium that's *too* successful. Such a publication or program will attract many ads and yours may not stand out in such a saturated environment. At the same time, you also don't want a medium offering such riveting editorial content that your ad is ignored, a concern that may explain the mundane nature of so much television programming.

For many people, money alone is the difference between advertising and media marketing. The only problem with this quick and neat distinction is accuracy: "Free" promotion is an illusion.

Although media coverage may be free, obtaining such exposure is not. Whether you do it yourself or hire professionals, generating worthwhile media exposure takes time, preparation and considerable thought.

If media marketing is not free, then how much is it worth? Why can't you place a price tag on media marketing efforts by calculating the cost for equivalent advertising space? Suppose you can buy advertising space at $100 per column inch in a metropolitan daily; shouldn't a 15-inch story be valued at $1,500?

In statistical terms it's certainly possible to calculate the value of media coverage if our standard is raw space and airtime. The problem, however, is that we're attempting to compare radically different concepts.

Advertising is unfiltered communication that allows you to control the content of your message. Short of libel, unproven medical claims or bigotry, you can say whatever you want, and most media outlets will run your ad untouched. With media marketing, you rely on journalists to interpret your story.

Advertising allows you to place an ad any day or, if you like, every day. For a premium, you can often ensure which page or section will carry your ad. With media marketing, it's impossible to project when or if an article will appear, or when and whether a broadcast will air. Worse still, even if you obtain coverage, you can't be sure what will be presented; you have no control over the length, content, style, placement or context of whatever is being printed or broadcast.

The distinctions between advertising and media marketing seem to give a significant edge to advertising. But there is another value to consider: the nature of communication.

Advertising is an adversarial form of contact. Someone is trying to sell something and no matter how well presented, advertising is advertising. Even so-called institutional advertisements—the messages that tell us to drive safer, drink less or give more to charity—are adversarial in the sense that advertisers seek to enhance their names by associating with a particular public concern. If institutional efforts are meant as purely munificent gestures, then surely there is no reason why such ads can't be anonymous.

Media marketing is not an adversarial form of communication, precisely because it's filtered through independent journalists and their editors or news directors. The public reads, watches and listens with the expectation that working journalists have gathered the news for us. If they write or broadcast information about a particular subject, we assume there must be some news value in the topic. News articles and broadcasts are not perceived as places where goods and services are sold or as forums where coverage can be bought, and therefore information that appears in the news is not regarded as adversarial communication.

Suppose a bank spends $10,000 advertising a new certificate of deposit (CD) in a local business section and receives 150 responses. Suppose also that a columnist writes about the CD and the result is 800 queries.

Is it possible the firm's ads are merely ineffective? Sure. Another reason, however, is that people resist salesmanship. The very act of selling, in and of itself, causes us to raise our defenses. But since news articles and broadcasts are not commonly perceived as marketing tools, the public has no reason to be defensive, and therefore a major barrier to acceptance is removed.

A Practical Example

The strength of commonsense promotional programs can be easily tested by looking at the results achieved by firms that do little or no advertising.

John Gornall, a noted marketing consultant, tells this story in his monthly newsletter, *The Housing Executive Report* (P.O. Box 911, Millsboro, DE 19966).

Over a two-year period, says Gornall, the Charles Cudd Company of Woodbury, Minnesota, spent $22.50 on advertising. Despite this virtually invisible ad budget, the firm sells 70, $200,000 homes annually. The secret? A good product is central to the company's success. But in addition, the company has a simple, but effective customer-relations program.

"During the construction process," writes Gornall, "salespeople call *every customer* once a week and update them. Every Friday afternoon each job in process is reviewed by sales and construction personnel. A list of *every* Cudd customer in the past two years is *given* to each prospective buyer. Customers are encouraged to talk to previous Cudd customers."

Is Cudd using media marketing concepts? You bet. It has defined its public and found an effective way to communicate with it.

Advertising tells the world how you want to be regarded, but when you're the subject of press attention, it's seen as the media making an evaluation. With positive editorial coverage from an independent media outlet, you gain the implicit, undeniable sanction and approval of the publication or program that carries your story, an entitlement that cannot be valued in the same way that we price column inches or airtime.

WHAT IS NEWS?

Trying to define the term *news* is somewhat like watching a magician pulling scarves from a thimble. First, there is a small wisp of color and soon yards and yards of material follow. The concept of *news* is equally baffling: What seems clear and obvious up-front turns out to be surprisingly complex.

Knowing how to define *news* is not merely an academic exercise; it's essential for those wanting press coverage. The media has an innate interest in news and it follows that if what you're doing or saying is *news*, the media will also have an interest in you. But what is news?

Perhaps the best way to test the news value of a particular story is to paraphrase an ancient question: What makes a person, event, product, idea or organization different from all others? Information without distinction is data, not news.

News, in the most basic sense, is simply information you didn't have before. When you first hear the local football team is ahead 21 to 6 in the third quarter or that your favorite hardware store was robbed, that's news.

But if it's true that *news* is fresh information, it's also true that some news is both known and aged. On New Year's Day, you can find any number of year-in-review reports telling you things you already know. Weekly and monthly magazines routinely recount "old" news, albeit with information and perspectives that may not have been available at the time of the event. Reporters rewrite old information and create background pieces, so breaking news ("new" news?) can be seen in perspective. A given event can produce ten different stories, each with a different perspective oriented toward a specific audience. Commentators take old information, add their opinions and create columns and editorials. These commentaries, in turn, may evolve into news by raising new ideas and perspectives.

Whether old or new, news is also information tailored to a specific audience or "public." Suppose a plane crashes at a major metropolitan airport. That information may make the local paper's front page. The same accident could also create a business article detailing the finances of the plane's corporate owners; a regulatory article discussing how governmental agencies are responding—or have responded in the past—to the type of problem that caused the crash; an airline safety feature in a major national magazine; a review of airplane claims processing in an insurance magazine; a first-person account in a monthly magazine; a feature on airport disaster services in a medical journal; ongoing daily and weekly broadcast accounts as the accident is investigated over time; and a discussion of how the media covers crashes in a journalism review.

So now we can define news as new information, old information, repackaged information, expanded or condensed information, information that's the subject of commentary, personalized information, time-sensitive information, information placed in context, entertaining information, information oriented toward a specific audience and information that for one reason or another is considered unique to a particular audience. In essence, the concept of news is so wondrously elastic that almost any information is news somewhere. But if virtually every smidgen of information can be defined as news, why are so few promotional efforts successful?

Although information per se can be news, for a story to be usable it must also offer *utility*, *placement* and *packaging*.

Utility means contacting the right media outlet at the right time. A new product that blocks excessive sun tanning is likely to draw little attention with a February news release in Buffalo. It's potentially news, but it's not particularly useful. The same story in Tampa might make a general, medical or business feature at any time of year.

Even if a news release has news value, that value shrinks to zero if the release is sent to the wrong publication or station. Placement counts, and it pays to carefully examine each media contact before sending out releases. If a local college just raised $15 million to build a new gym, that may be news for local media or an alumni publication. But for a forestry magazine, chemical industry newsletter or city magazine 200 miles away, the story is likely to land in the dumper.

Most importantly, news values can be defined long before a news release is ever mailed. In creating media materials, individuals and organizations can strongly influence their promotional potential by the way they package stories.

Seven Ways To Build a Story

It's always news when the circus comes to town or a new teenage spelling champ is proclaimed, even though everyone has heard these stories before. Such events are newsworthy only because promoters have taken standardized stories and added a little spice, a new twist and some updating to make them current. Here are seven quick ways to embellish potential stories.

Does it conflict? Disagreements, court battles, disputes, discord, splits and divisions all make good stories.

Is it extreme? The mundane and the usual become newsworthy when the right adjectives are added. We're interested in things and events that are larger, smaller, longer, wider, heavier, lighter, first, last, faster, slower, younger and older. The shortest guy in the NBA and the biggest convention in town both get coverage.

Is it dated? Is it happening now, later, tomorrow or never? Currency makes news and events related to a given date can also be newsworthy. A newly discovered set of Lincoln's papers will make headlines. Bigger headlines are possible if the discovery is announced on the Great Emancipator's birthday.

Consider this example. Mr. Fulton, a real estate broker, lists the largest home in town, a property known as Walmouth Manor. He can send out a news release announcing his new listing and then rely on various reporters to find a suitable angle to make the story newsworthy. Journalists, however, can choose from lots of good stories. If Fulton is shrewd, he will make his story more competitive by offering a fresh angle to each reporter.

Different angles, or news "pegs," can be used to promote Fulton's listing to separate publics; that is, locally ("Fulton Lists City's Most Expensive Home"), regionally ("Record High Marks County Home Sale"), as a consumer story ("Lux-

---

Seven Ways To Build a Story (continued)

Is it a milestone? We relate to markers such as the town's 100th anniversary, the one millionth album and the score of the last game. Give a story a milestone and you've created a news peg.

Is it localized? Floods in our home town are news; floods in Peru are less interesting. The floods, and the potential for tragedy, are identical, but location influences our interest level.

Is it specialized? Does it affect a particular profession, religion, club or industry? We are each unique, but we are each part of many publics. The Methodist carpenter who collects stamps and vacations in Bermuda is part of at least four identifiable groupings: Methodists, carpenters, stamp collectors and Caribbean vacationers. An event that touches one of these four special interests may be newsworthy to him, but perhaps less so to the Catholic attorney who bowls weekly and vacations in Canada. The attorney has her own set of special interests.

Does it help? Devise a story that tells people "how to" and you'll get coverage. Favorites include how to save money, make money, lose weight, find romance, stay healthy, be popular, keep fit and stay young.

---

ury House Has Features for Every Buyer"), for a local business newspaper ("Fulton Says Big Listing Means Big Year"), as a local feature ("Cancer Group Holds Ball at Walmouth Manor"), for a national industry publication ("How To List the Biggest Home in Town") or as a feature for homeowners ("Gardening Secrets from Walmouth Manor"). For the local broadcast media, one could easily see Fulton conducting a tour on daytime TV or discussing the real estate marketplace on radio call-in programs.

By segmenting his market and packaging his appeals, Fulton's story can attract greater media coverage than would be possible with a single, all-purpose news release. For Fulton, or for you, properly defining and packaging stories before they

Authority Figures

While packaging is part of the promotion game, another part depends on the status of the packager. "Authority figures," people who can be identified in some way, are important in journalism because covering, quoting or citing them gives depth and credibility to stories. The "person on the street" and the "family from Peoria" represent the common people. The company president, the elected official, the college professor, the society-ball chairperson, the town doctor, the union leader, the minister, the rabbi and the judge all receive regular coverage because of their positions and constituencies.

What if you're not a doctor or elected official? Can you still be an authority figure?

The role of authority figure is an equal-opportunity position: everyone qualifies or can qualify.

To be an authority figure there must be some reason why you're quotable. If it happens that you don't have a law degree or high position in industry, don't worry. It's OK to create your own credentials. For instance, contribute to an industry journal or self-publish booklets and pamphlets. You'll have a quotable something to send reporters.

Give a speech. Speeches convey an element of authority and importance. Speaking engagements are available everywhere, all the time. Try clubs, associations, professional societies and industry groups for speaking dates. You'll need a cover letter and program outline to get booked.

Letters to the editor are popular, well read and sure to attract media attention. Be brief, concentrate on one subject, quote sources to back up your viewpoint and criticize, if appropriate, in a respectful manner.

Teach. Give courses and seminars through community groups, professional organizations, adult education services, junior colleges and noncredit schools. There's a constant search for good instructors, people with real-world experience and solid teaching skills.

Last, *get stationery,* call a few friends and create your own organization. If you're unhappy with the latest phone rate increases, it's easier to get coverage if you're president of the Northside Telephone Users or the Southlawn Citizens Association than if you're a lone telephone user.

reach reporters is a decided advantage in the fight for media time and attention.

HOW BIG FIRMS GET COVERAGE

There aren't many days when the news is not dominated by massive organizations. When a large corporation opens a new factory, the Red Cross seeks blood, a union strikes or the local government raises taxes, many people are affected and by definition such events are news.

That giant organizations are well covered by the media is hardly surprising. Much of our news concerns events and activities only large enterprises can organize or develop. Stories about a $700-million chemical plant are likely to feature gargantuan corporations rather than minor subcontractors.

In the competition for media time and attention, large organizations often enjoy continuing media access not because they are big, but because they can be readily covered by the media. And immediate access, in turn, is a fundamental consideration in the process of choosing stories.

Suppose a plane crashes in Washington, killing 30 people. On the same day, a mine disaster in a remote Montana valley results in an equal number of deaths. Both are terrible tragedies, but you can be certain the plane crash will draw far more attention.

Why? Because the Washington crash offers immediate access. The nation's capital is a major media center and so nearby reporters and camera crews can be routed to the crash site in minutes. Film can be developed and edited immediately while reporters on the scene provide live updates as new information is received.

As for the mine disaster, it surely deserves coverage, but it takes so long to send cameras and reporters to the scene that the element of immediacy is lost. Even though "long" may be just a few hours in this example, in the competition for media time and space, the mine disaster loses. Figure the Montana accident for extensive local coverage, but elsewhere it will rate a short story on day one, a follow-up with photo on day two and possibly a few paragraphs in a national newsmagazine a week later, perhaps as the lead for a general article on mine safety.

In less dramatic fashion, large organizations also offer immediate access. They arrange their affairs so that reporters can easily obtain information, interviews, files and photos on short notice. Knowledgeable media contacts employed by major organizations—often former journalists—keep reporters abreast of new developments, respond to media inquiries and suggest story ideas. Some organizations even advertise their availability as sources and list company contacts in media journals.

To see how immediate access works on a practical basis, consider the case of a real estate reporter writing about local housing trends. There are hundreds of area realty companies, and a reporter could look in the phone book, pick names at random and see what different brokers might say. And although such random calls can occur, the reporter also knows that three major firms with active media information operations dominate the local market, each maintains extensive sales reports and each has a knowledgeable, quotable spokesman who can discuss current sales trends.

How did the reporter know about the company studies or whom to contact? Several reasons stand out.

- One presumes large firms in certain fields have specialized information relating to their own activities.

- Large firms routinely have information specialists who contact journalists and make sure reporters know what the company is doing. The very effort to reach the media, in and of itself, influences news coverage.

- It's easier and quicker to call three known sources who understand how to work with the media than to unearth new contacts at random, particularly when deadlines loom.

- Not contacting large firms in a given field could result in a weak or incomplete story.

- Journalists who regularly cover individual "beats" such as housing, insurance, securities or banking develop sources over time and know who is a good contact and who isn't. Such companies have probably been sources in the past.

- Reporters may have heard or seen information elsewhere and are now following up with their own stories.

Although the "immediate" access created by large organizations seems to benefit both reporter and subject, the process contains two sizable flaws.

First, many large organizations have articulate, professional information specialists who constantly update reporters. Indeed, information from such sources is so voluminous that some journalists can probably sit back and cover certain industries just on the basis of handouts they receive.

But continually getting information from a limited number of sources creates a problem: If reporters use too much material from one source—even if that information is the best available—readers, listeners and viewers may wonder where the reportorial effort begins and the company information program ends, or how one can tell the difference between the two.

Second, although "immediate" access is convenient, often helpful and certainly the right approach for firms and organizations, the term *immediate* should not be confused with "complete" or "unbiased" access.

For general stories to be accurate, fair and in context, it takes more information—and viewpoints—than a single source can readily provide. Conversely, if immediate access does nothing more than allow large organizations, or anyone, to gain a hearing for their views, that's a substantial advantage in the battle for media time and attention.

IS THERE ROOM FOR THE LITTLE GUY?

With all the resources commanded by large companies, big associations and huge governmental agencies, it would seem as though individuals and small organizations could not compete for media attention. After all, don't big organizations dominate the media if only because they're so large?

In a word, no.

Every year *Fortune* magazine identifies the 500 largest American companies, the very organizations that should dominate the media, if domination were possible, on the basis of size, resources and influence. But how many *Fortune* 500 firms can you name? Suppose you stop 100 people on the street and showed them the *Fortune* list. How many could identify the principal products or services offered by individual companies?

There is a somewhat perverse reality concerning large organizations and the media. Although corporate giants, unions, government and other institutions receive extensive press attention, one can argue that general media coverage is remarkably limited considering the players involved.

Suppose General Widget, a $5 billion conglomerate with 32 factories in 11 states, increases sales by 12 percent. A news release goes out, but what gets into print? Maybe a paragraph or two in business sections or just a single line in a list of corporate earnings. What gets on radio or TV? Five seconds on a business report or maybe nothing.

What's the problem?

Large organizations often have little to offer reporters besides their size. They've grown big over many years doing things that in many cases are not new ("We built the Cloverdale Works in 1903..."), innovative ("We've been making the #407 widget for 36 years...") or particularly understandable to anyone outside the industry ("The reverse camber rod flexes inversely when the glombar decelerates, causing the rear fleenstones to twist laterally...").

There are many General Widgets in the world and they often compete for attention in a limited number of national media outlets. With so much competition and so little space, it's obvious that not everyone will receive coverage.

General Widget—with its excellent information program and media contacts—is always there. A journalist who cannot find information and ideas from other sources can always go back to a General Widget.

Individuals and small organizations, however, are rarely beset by the problems above. Being small often means being new, innovative and highly competitive. Similar companies or organizations may exist elsewhere, but within a given area or industry a small firm can be unique.

Small businesses are often at the heart of terrific stories. Would you rather read about companies closing and factories laying off workers or about new technologies and prosperous entrepreneurs? Small organizations must be doing something right. According to *The State of Small Business: A Report of the President,* firms in industries dominated by small businesses added 1.03 million new jobs to the work force between September 1988 and September 1989. Industries dominated by large companies, firms with more than 500 employees, accounted for an increase of just 248,000 positions.

The media, for its part, loves to hear from individuals and small organizations. For journalists dealing with individuals and small businesses, however, it's hard to tell who represents a good story and who doesn't. There may be 5,000 small organizations in an area or industry, but do reporters really have the time to call each one?

If you're a professional or have a small business, you might want to help those periodicals and stations that might *reasonably* have an interest in you or your ideas, products or services. It's okay to send a brief letter to a few journalists, something that says, "If it ever happens that you do a story about my product (or service or industry or whatever), we may be able to provide (information, a plant tour, statistics, reports, a lively interview, and so on). We've been in the business for 14 years (or "We've developed a new technology" or "I'm the president of an industry group" or "We're the largest broker in town" and so on) and we may be a useful source when it comes time to develop a story. Please feel free to call."

Given a choice between calling old sources time and again or new sources who may offer different perspectives, journalists will be open to new contacts. After all, the very fact that there is a new source may justify or validate an otherwise mundane story in a business always looking for something new, something different and something unique.

How a Small Business Grew

When Pamela Barefoot started the Blue Crab Bay Co. from her kitchen in 1985, her idea was to gather the handmade products of Virginia's rural Eastern Shore, package an assortment of jams, jellies and seafood in handmade baskets, and then market the baskets as unique gift items. To promote her baskets Barefoot printed 2,000 brochures, but the brochures resulted in just 30 sales.

Poor sales were not the only problem Barefoot encountered. An accident kept her in traction for two months, a hurricane damaged her house, and when she moved her operation above Hopkin's Store—an area landmark on a small Chesapeake Bay creek—the building caught fire within two days and Barefoot promptly moved back to the relative safety of her home.

Between poor sales and acts of nature, many would-be entrepreneurs would have quit. But Barefoot took a different tack, wrote about her experiences and entered a national essay contest sponsored by *SELF* magazine. She won a $7,500 prize as well as attention that led to coverage in food, business and trade publications.

Barefoot's business has grown to the point where she serves wholesale clients as well as 1,000 food and gift shops in the United States and Canada. In addition, Barefoot now has a retail store in Onancock and a catalog for her mail-order business (Blue Crab Bay Company, 57 Market Street, Onancock, VA 23417; 804-787-3602).

Has media exposure helped?

"A lot of shops carry our products because they have heard or read about our product," says Barefoot. "It's given us product identity."

2

How To Deal
with Reporters

While the advantages of media attention are attractive—at least on occasion—contacting reporters may seem strange and foreign. In a society where tooting one's horn is seen in a negative context, calling or writing a total stranger to promote oneself or one's story may seem pushy, egocentric and tasteless.

There is also the problem of who you're contacting. Don't reporters spend their time muckraking? Aren't they the folks who unearth scandals, find government waste and televise shoddy business practices? If you phone or write a reporter, won't you get nosy questions in return?

As with any profession, reporters have certain obligations to those they serve, but with journalism such obligations are often obscured by public perceptions. We tend to see the glamour of journalism rather than the grinding realities. At best, much of journalism can be described as labor-intensive—there is nothing exciting about attending lengthy hearings, reading voluminous files or making dozens of phone calls while researching stories.

Then, of course, few professions are subject to such intense public scrutiny. Critics are everywhere and not all are particularly lucid. At least one radio talk show host has been gunned down in the last few years.

What can you expect when dealing with reporters? Will reporters listen to your ideas or will you be ignored? Here are several observations.

Don't expect to speak with a secretary. Print reporters typically answer their own phones, do their own typing and open their own mail. You can speak with just about any writer directly, but neither a postage stamp nor the cost of a phone call earns you an unlimited commitment of journalistic time or attention. Access to television reporters, particularly anchor personnel, is more restricted.

Don't worry about enlightened self-promotion. If you've got an idea that can be a good story and it happens coincidentally that you benefit, that's not a problem. If your idea is entirely self-serving, don't plan a long conversation.

Don't expect to see a story before it's run. If a subject is technical and complex, the reporter will either be competent enough to handle the topic or will ask for clarification. Remember that journalists often cover regular beats or work for specialized publications. They have ongoing access to experts in every field, and by virtue of their training and experience many are regarded as authorities in their own right.

Be patient. Recognize that the publication or broadcast of "feature" material—stories not time-sensitive like breaking news—will often be delayed.

Work with a reporter on his or her turf. With large publications do not expect a reporter on one beat to write about a topic usually covered by someone else. Turf and territory are important. The same proposition holds true at radio and TV stations as well.

Consider the nature of the reporter's work. Competition in journalism is ongoing and universal, a process sometimes called "creative tension." Journalistic competition includes not

The Myth of Perfect Objectivity

In the mid-1980s Senator Jesse Helms (R-NC) and a group called Fairness in Media asked "almost one million" conservatives to invest their dollars in CBS stock and elect corporate directors who would "put an end to liberal media bias."

Regardless of whether one agrees with Helms, his proposal raises complex issues. Was, or is, CBS News liberal? If so, what is "liberal"? If by some standard we can describe "liberal," and if CBS News is liberal, how exactly would this affect news judgments? Would news stories be more "biased" or less biased if CBS News were "conservative," assuming someone could explain what *conservative* means? What would it take for TV news to be "objective" and who is to define that term? How, in practice, does *objective* differ from *liberal* or *conservative?*

Throughout American history there have been avowed political publications and in a sense the Helms effort to take over CBS follows in this tradition. As examples, William Lloyd Garrison (1805–1879) published the *Liberator*, a paper opposed to slavery. William Randolph Hearst (1863–1951) used his papers to encourage the Spanish-American War. Today, publications favoring a variety of political, social, economic and religious viewpoints are available in every community.

At some point in every field there must be a person who makes decisions, who has responsibility. We have judges who review laws, doctors who recommend treatments and also we have journalists who define what's news for a particular publication or program and what isn't.

No one argues that the decisions made by journalists are perfect or can be perfect, however one defines *perfection*. News reporting is a subjective field where many views are possible, one reason we have so many media outlets. But journalism should be left to journalists, however imperfect, rather than business tycoons, political theorists or other vested interests. One may not always agree with the judgments made by independent reporters, but at least such decisions are not made with other obligations in mind.

only external battles—one magazine versus another or one radio station against a second station—but also internal fights among individuals, staffs and sections. Success is measured by prestige assignments, column inches, airtime and placement. If you've got a story that will lead page one, the reporter who writes it will look good to colleagues and peers—at least for a day. Conversely, the reporter who does great work for a year and is then less productive can be fired. There may be tenure in teaching and job security in many fields, but journalism isn't one of them.

Remember: The reporter is not omnipotent.   Recognize that the editorial process is complex and that the interest of a single reporter may not ensure coverage. A local television station, for instance, may have assignment editors, reporters, anchors and producers involved in the decision to use a particular item. Their preferences may be delayed or overturned if a hot story breaks, an executive producer dislikes the topic or a camera crew isn't available.

When you talk, others listen.   Don't be surprised if you hear from a variety of people as a result of media coverage. Some will love what you say while others will think you're subversive. Prospective purchasers will want your product while competitors will wonder how you got coverage and they didn't. Then there will be individuals who feel that since you received media attention, you're a rousing success and therefore obligated to finance their favorite charity. Most importantly, reporters constantly check competing media, a process called "research," so you're likely to receive calls from other journalists as a result of one article or broadcast.

You're a seller in a buyer's market.   Be aware that even though you may have spent time with a reporter, been interviewed and supplied information, it doesn't obligate a reporter to use your material, accept your views or do a story.

If You Want Copies

Don't expect reporters to send copies of articles or interviews. The presumption is that you normally read, listen to or watch their work so there is no need for them to make copies. On the other hand...

Reporters for distant publications not available locally will often mail clips as a matter of courtesy. It helps to supply a stamped, self-addressed envelope.

Radio hosts will often make a program cassette, especially if you ask.

Television producers, for some reason, rarely supply videos. The only solution here is to show up for a program with your own blank tape and to then ask the producer to make a copy. Most will agree.

Receiving a copy of a report in which you are featured should not be seen as a license to reproduce the material or to use it commercially. If you want more than courtesy, be certain to obtain appropriate permission in writing.

RULES FOR MEDIA MARKETING

Every profession and industry has a particular way of doing business, a series of standards and approaches that distinguish "insiders" from the rest of the world. If you're in the field, you know where the boundaries are, what constitutes professionally appropriate behavior and where corners can be cut.

In the relationship between journalists and promoters, there are also unwritten understandings, caveats that can be divided into three major groups: do's, don'ts and cautions.

Do's are actions, or non-actions, entirely acceptable within journalism. No one will be offended if you write a letter proposing a story idea, even if the idea isn't usable.

Don'ts are taboos, steps to avoid if you want either credibility or coverage. Including $100 bills with a news release may ensure media attention, but it's not likely to be the kind of attention you might enjoy.

The third category of behavior, *cautions,* represent situations where there are no universally accepted norms. You need to act thoughtfully in such cases because it's entirely possible to needlessly offend someone if you don't.

For instance, who pays if you and a journalist have lunch? You? The reporter? Do you share the bill? The answer may depend on who invited whom, the journalist's comfort level with you, the topics discussed and where the meeting is held. The answer may also depend on the reporter's employer. Some news organizations have no rules on the subject while others strictly limit business lunches and other matters, not because they think reporters will be corrupted, but because they worry that such meetings may create a perception of impropriety or obligation.

If the bill comes and you're unsure how it should be handled, it's always fair to say, "I'll be happy to pick up the tab, but I know some organizations have rules about luncheons. Would it be better for us to split the bill? You tell me what's best." Now the issue has been recognized and the reporter can comfortably suggest a solution.

Here, in brief, are a variety of do's, don'ts and cautions to consider.

PROMOTIONAL DO'S

To the extent possible, tailor your efforts to individual reporters and media outlets.   All media outlets, even those competing in the same field or for the same audience, have distinct needs and interests. An idea unacceptable at one outlet may be a lead story elsewhere. The bad news is that because media interests differ, a single, universal pitch sent to hundreds of media outlets will have a very low rate of success.

Journalism is a tough, competitive business and reporters earn no medals duplicating coverage. If your story is important, if you want maximum consideration, customize your proposal for each outlet and reporter you contact.

Customizing materials may seem tedious and time-consuming and so the question often arises: Should every story idea be customized? The answer depends on the subject's importance. The more important to you, the more customizing is in order. The less important, the more appropriate to churn out standardized news releases (and the less likely they'll receive serious attention).

Journalists are forever in the position of making judgments, trying to decide what's important and what isn't. If you want media attention, if you believe something is significant, then you need to spend time thinking about the needs of individual reporters and media outlets. If a story idea only rates a standardized news release, you've so much as said your news isn't especially important. If it were, then surely you'd take the time to say why. In effect, deciding whether to customize materials strongly influences editorial judgments.

When appropriate, send more than a news release. Some ideas cannot be adequately explored in a single news release. When faced with a complex subject, successful promoters provide supporting materials such as fact sheets that briefly outline story concepts, question-and-answer dialogues to address complex issues that cannot be discussed within the space of a news release and background statements or histories to give perspective and show why a story is important.

Graphics are another item to send. Charts, tables and photos can all be valuable. Make certain your graphic is properly identified ("Source: The Woodwell Cooperative") so that you get full credit for your work.

Maintain credibility. The central measure in journalism is credibility, a fragile value that must be upheld in each article or broadcast. A reporter's words and information must be reliable; his or her public must be able to count on what is being written or said.

In a similar fashion, promoters must also be credible. No one will be surprised if you have a point of view or a bias; that's expected from promoters. But information presented to the media must be *truthful*, complete and in context, standards that apply not only to news releases but to interviews and supporting documents as well.

Build perception.   In the battle for media turf, perception can be as important as reality. And perception—like bridges and dams—can be engineered.

When the President's Commission on Organized Crime issued a report favoring widespread drug testing for government employees, there was considerable debate. No one, explained proponents, would want an air-traffic controller to land planes while under the influence of drugs. Those who opposed the idea said it was unworkable, unconstitutional, unreliable and a gross invasion of privacy.

Whatever the merits of either view, proponents lost an important battle when one of their leaders was surprised in public. At a congressional hearing filled with reporters and television cameras, a top commission staffer was asked to not only submit his words, but also some vital fluids—in the presence of a witness, just as government employees might be required under the commission's proposal. The bureaucrat refused and the undeniable public perception was clear: If a top commission staffer wouldn't agree to a surprise test, why should anyone else?

Become a source.   As journalists gain experience, they develop a network of regular sources on whom they rely for information, ideas and opinions. Such sources may be quoted in print or on the air, but in many cases they supply information on a "background" basis; that is, without public attribution. Many associations, for example, make researchers, specialists and librarians available to reporters on a background basis.

Initially, it may seem as though not getting public recognition defeats the entire purpose of promotion. After all, isn't media marketing supposed to generate media exposure? Why help reporters if you're not being publicized?

First, if you're a source, you're credible. A journalist won't bother calling if you're not reliable.

Second, as a source, you're influential. The reason a reporter calls is because a story is not complete. More information, ideas and perspectives are needed and whatever you provide can influence the ultimate content and context of a story.

Third, when seeking coverage, sources have direct access to the media since they're familiar and have proved reliable in the past.

Be aware of deadlines.   Journalism is a time-sensitive industry with such products as the 6 P.M. news, the morning paper and the December magazine.

Formulate campaigns so media outlets will have enough time to consider and possibly cover your story. If you're aiming for March magazine coverage and the publications you want to reach are assigning stories for that issue in November and December of the prior year, it's easy to see that advance planning is necessary.

Time sensitivity is another aspect of deadline awareness. If a daily reporter has a 3 P.M. deadline, don't even think of a 2 P.M. chitchat. Not only won't the conversation be lengthy, but future contacts are likely to be chilled. It's okay to start a conversation with a simple question: "Is this a good time?"

Identify other sources.   Because few stories have just one side, reporters want a variety of viewpoints. If you've got the names, addresses and phone numbers of people who might make good sources, that can be valuable information to pass on to a reporter, particularly if some of your sources are competitors or oppose your views.

It may seem as though identifying alternative sources defeats the purpose of media marketing. Why should you help someone else receive press coverage, especially a competitor or opponent?

One reason is that a story will have greater value, and thus a better chance of being used, if it has balance. Another reason is that an enterprising journalist will speak to a variety of sources anyway, so why not provide names and numbers upfront? A third reason is that without conflict there may not be a story.

Have perspective.   There are products that can objectively be described as "new and improved," but how many are utterly perfect? How many times is there only one approach to a given problem?

If your story concept is good, if your idea is compelling, then it should be open to discussion and criticism. Not only does open debate make for a better story, it also demonstrates an essential strength, character and dimension that makes something, or someone, newsworthy and credible.

As an example, in the early 1970s a small manufacturer used a laser to place tiny holes in contact lenses. The lenses enabled certain patients to wear their lenses longer and in greater comfort.

In developing a media strategy, the company wrote a history showing the evolution of contact lenses dating back to da Vinci. It had a one-page news release that announced the new lens, but the release very carefully stated that while the lenses benefited certain patients, they were not valuable for all. The only way individuals could determine if the lenses were right for them was to see an "eye-care professional." This approach produced several interesting results.

First, because the company freely admitted that the lenses were not the most wonderful invention since Ben Franklin's bifocals, it had credibility.

Second, the company did not want to be in the position of creating false hopes for people with acute eye problems. Its conservative posture, its willingness to acknowledge the limitations of its product, also created credibility.

Third, few reporters knew the history of contact lenses or that da Vinci is widely regarded as their inventor. The history gave perspective and dimension to the story, made it something more than just a health products feature.

Fourth, by telling people to consult with individual "eye-care professionals," the company accomplished two goals. It properly sent prospective patients to optometrists, opticians and ophthalmologists for individual attention. It also avoided being aligned with optometrists, opticians or ophthalmologists, three groups that sometimes compete for the same patients.

Correct mistakes.   People make mistakes. Organizations make mistakes. Journalists make mistakes. Mistakes being entirely common, why not say so?

Journalists do not expect the people they interview to have the linguistic skills of an Oxford don. Reporters want accuracy but they recognize that a media interview is not a pop quiz.

Interviews can make people nervous and nervous people can forget information, invert words or ramble with something less than their usual coherence. If you find that in the midst of an interview you goofed, say so. If the interview is finished and you realize a mistake was made, call the reporter back as quickly as possible. Print copy can often be corrected before it goes to press, radio tapes can also be edited in many cases, but the situation with TV is more difficult. It's unlikely that a TV station will send out a camera crew twice or that an interview program will have a second "take" once taping is finished. At best, hope that errant TV material is edited, cut or not used.

Name a contact. In large organizations there should be one central office or media-wise person to expedite press inquiries, arrange interviews and locate information. This is a common arrangement for mid-size and large corporations, associations and governmental agencies.

Many business, civic and social groups, however, handle media relations by naming their president as the media contact. This is a "benefit" of leadership, a practice that assumes organizational leaders can speak knowledgeably to the media.

There are often problems when the president, being president, tries to deal with all the media inquiries received by the group. For instance, a local bankers' organization may be headed by someone with experience in consumer lending, a problem when questions concerning long-term bonds or personal banking arise.

An alternative for groups is to develop an experts' list. Poll the membership, find out who's interested in what, make up a roster with several names under each heading, and then distribute the list to the media. The very fact that there is such a list may suggest story ideas and new contacts.

Assume you're on the record. Unless you have a clear agreement to the contrary, whenever you speak with a journalist assume that your name and information will be used in a story

---

What To Do in a Crisis

Groups and individuals in the news are often remarkably accessible until problems arise. Then, suddenly, people aren't in, calls aren't returned, and folks who once burned up the phone lines looking for coverage disappear.

The "take to the hills" response to bad news cedes all promotional ground to one's adversaries and critics. There's no possibility of defending your position or explaining what went wrong. Every group, corporation and organization needs a crisis management plan and part of that plan must include a willingness to speak with the media.

The 1982 Tylenol poisonings in Chicago illustrate the best way to handle an emergency. Here drug capsules had been laced with cyanide and several people died. In full view of the public, the manufacturer removed capsules from store shelves nationwide and took back capsules purchased by consumers. The cost to the company may have been as high as $250 million, a staggering expense. But not much later Tylenol was back in the market as a best-selling painkiller. The public saw that the manufacturer had acted fairly and quickly, that it was willing to take tremendous losses to protect its customers and that it too was a victim. A potential boondoggle was turned around, in large measure by the manufacturer's willingness to deal openly with a terrible problem and by the widespread sense of trust that resulted.

---

and that whatever you say will appear in print. *Given this perspective, watch what you say.*

Feedback is important.   With feedback, whether positive or negative, a journalist can decide whether to continue coverage of a given subject, change his or her approach or drop the matter completely. If you receive coverage, wait a few days and then call or write the reporter and say what happened because of the story.

Feedback is not only valuable for reporters, it's also important for promoters, a way to stay in touch that's not contrived, artificial or adversarial.

PROMOTIONAL DON'TS

Avoid blanket mailings.   Sending releases to six reporters at the same outlet and at the same time in the hopes of coverage by each can be a disaster. In the worst possible case, each reporter will develop a story, the stories will be printed on the same day in different sections of the paper and you will never again appear on the pages of that publication.

Don't socialize excessively.   Journalism is a business and while there are times when it's appropriate to socialize with reporters, such moments are limited. Certainly promoters should not call reporters to talk about the weather or gossip as a way to induce media coverage.

Don't relate advertising to editorial coverage.   The purchase of advertising is a marketing decision that should be made on the ability of a publication or station to reach a particular audience at a given cost. Conversely, advertising alone should not be a bar to editorial coverage.

While some media outlets *do* relate advertising to what they call editorial coverage, it's clear that the most desirable publications and programs do not. The value of editorial coverage is based on credibility and there isn't much that's credible when ties with advertisers are obvious and overt. If you're going to contact reporters associated with independent media outlets, forget about advertising. At best, the subject places an unhealthy pall over any contacts you may develop; at worst—and most likely—your conversation will end abruptly.

CAUTIONS

Don't expect journalists to be your promoters. Except for advocacy forums such as editorials and signed columns, a journalist's only obligation in news stories and broadcasts is to present information and ideas to a given public fairly, accurately and in context.

Don't believe that friendship is a substitute for a poor story. Rather than relying on personal relations with a reporter, editor or broadcaster to pitch a story, good promoters stress news values such as how a story will benefit the journalist's audience. Suggesting that a story should be used merely because a reporter is a neighbor, buddy or golfing partner demeans the journalist's integrity.

Avoid promotional excesses. The most important promotional inducement is simply information. Meals, tours, samples, trips, etc., must be viewed as possibly inappropriate and handled with extreme care.

Is a luncheon or sample excessive in a given promotional effort, or is a favor expected in return? For instance, if a reporter is going to be at a new industrial park all day, proposing lunch on-site or nearby seem reasonable. Driving 150 miles to the most expensive place in the state is inappropriate.

There are some businesses and activities where the line between appropriate and inappropriate promotion is hard to draw. If you're in the cruise business and you have a new ship, is it appropriate to suggest a story? Sure. Is it appropriate to pay for a reporter's room and board? That's not so clear. Some publications and stations will allow such arrangements, others will not. Those banning free trips will pay for a ticket if they elect to do a story.

Note, however, there are absolutists in the fourth estate who seriously worry about such galactic issues as free key chains and complimentary pens. The principal of journalists receiving goods of any value, not the tokens themselves, is a source of conflict. Yet somehow, magically, no one seems compromised by preferential postal rates for publications, the free use of space and facilities in government buildings or the value of all those spokesmen and spokeswomen and news releases that are the basis of so many stories and, in effect, represent an undeniable form of subsidy.

Because the issue of promotional items and services is so sensitive, because feelings are strong, promoters should tread carefully in this area. Always question if something of value—lunch, a token, a ride to the factory, whatever—is clearly related to a story. If not, forget it.

Avoid invective. It's easy to say things in conversation that look awful in print or sound terrible on the air. A good interview rule is be circumspect because you can't control the arena where your remarks will appear. You may feel a competitor is not on the up-and-up, but save that thought for private moments. Keep disagreements factual, explain why your case is strong and your opponent's is weak.

There are no guarantees in media marketing. The best efforts to promote a story can fail for reasons wholly outside the promoter's control. A story can be bumped to make room for another item or because an editor simply doesn't like the topic, the writing, the reporter's approach or a hundred other reasons. If you want guaranteed visibility, advertise.

Do the principles and protocols described here *guarantee* media coverage? Not at all. But it seems difficult to believe that one could follow these guidelines and not maximize such media attention as a story may deserve.

TEN WAYS TO KILL A STORY

With so many publications and broadcast stations looking for good stories, you'd think most promoters would have little trouble getting ideas in print or on the air. Yet many valid story concepts are never covered for the oddest of reasons: The promoter prevents coverage! This sounds like an utter contradiction of purpose and intent, but it happens more frequently than anyone might believe. Some practices make even the most

Libel and Slander

In America it's OK to have beliefs and viewpoints, including low opinions of other individuals, products and institutions. The catch is that some opinions can get you in trouble.

In general terms it's OK to express an opinion. If you think the food at Joe's Diner is miserable, you have the right to say so. If you're a food critic and say that Joe uses too much butter, and in fact Joe only uses margarine, then there can be problems.

Libel is usually seen as printed information that is untrue, defamatory and harmful. There are obvious libels (libel per se) such as a false claim that Smith is a convicted arsonist, and indirect libels (libel per quod) where, for example, it might be said that Jones associates with known mobsters, the inference being that Jones too is a criminal.

To show libel it is usually necessary for the plaintiff to at least prove that a report is untrue. There are exceptions for "public figures" such as actors and politicians, where malice must also be shown in many cases. Knowing that actress Jones loves animals and accidentally burned her cat is unlikely to be libelous. Saying that Jones purposely stuffed her cat in an oven would undoubtedly result in a libel suit.

Matters of opinion have traditionally been protected against libel suits, but in at least one case an opinion was ruled libelous because it was based on information the Supreme Court said was "false and defamatory."

In most instances individuals who are libeled do not bring suit against a publication and even when a suit is brought, most plaintiffs fail.

Rather than a court battle, people who feel they have been libeled typically ask for a retraction, something publications normally give if they are wrong. Even when a libel suit goes to court, and even when libel has been committed, plaintiffs are apt to collect small awards because it is difficult to prove economic damage.

In many situations when a libel occurs a hurt party will greatly prefer to forget the entire matter. The reason is that a retraction or a libel suit will just bring more attention to the false statements, something many plaintiffs wish to avoid.

Slander, by the way, is nothing more than an oral version of libel.

intriguing story excruciatingly difficult to develop and the result is that reporters move on to friendlier possibilities. Here are ten quick situations where promoters kill their own stories.

Situation 1: The uninformed spokesman. A firm's media contact has good relations with local reporters but management refuses to give him straight information about the company. Journalists ignore the company because its spokesman is not privy to the data they need. Guess who's fired because, says management, he can't get the firm's name in print?

Situation 2: The expert spokesman—and know-nothing staff. When reporters want information about Colossal Insurance all they need do is call Wanda Insight, the All-Knowing, Centralized Font of Insurance Knowledge, a virtual encyclopedia of industry news, prices, trends and history. But what happens when Insight is out to lunch, in a meeting, on leave or traveling? Can anyone else talk about the firm's sales in the past two years? "No," says Insight's assistant, "it's against company policy. Only Ms. Insight can speak to the media." When will she be in? "Next Tuesday. Maybe." You have to wonder how the company will survive if Insight is ever hit by a bus. Do reporters, unable to catch the elusive Ms. Insight, continue to call?

Situation 3: The censored CEO. A reporter has just spoken with the company president who is interesting, informative and quotable. Later the firm's media whiz calls to ask if more information is needed and casually mentions that one subject discussed by the company president is off-limits.

"You can't write about that subject," the reporter is told. "Mr. Mumbles (the firm's president) had no right to discuss that with you."

Really? How did Mumbles become president?

Situation 4: The copyrighted news release. A news release is sent to reporters marked "Copyright 1992 Invisible Management, Inc. All Rights Reserved. No part of this document may be quoted, reproduced or stored in whole or in part without

the express written permission of Invisible Management, Inc."
Does this mean a reporter must ask permission to use a news
release? Do you think many reporters will bother calling when
other stories await?

Situation 5: The too-important-for-words CEO.   The phone
rings and a voice asks, "Is Reporter Thompkins there? Could
you hold for Mr. H. Pickford Pickford, president of Pickford
Industries and a man so important he uses the same name
twice?" Is Mr. Pickford unable to dial, an invalid? Is there an
unsubtle hint that Mr. Pickford's time is more precious than
that of the reporter? Do reporters enjoy such intimations?

Situation 6: The not-so-exclusive interview.   Williams contacts magazine writer Bell with a story and promises not to say
anything to other reporters until Bell's piece appears in print.
Later, Bell is chagrined to see "her" story in the morning paper. Does writer Bell ever call Williams again?

Situation 7: "No questions, please."   The Pristine Pines Eco-
logical Paving and Concrete Company schedules a news conference to announce a new method of cobblestone extraction.
After the firm's president reads a statement he says, "There's
no sense in asking questions, all the information you need is in
your news kits" and walks away from the podium. Will you
read about Pristine Pines in the morning paper?

Situation 8: All talk, no backup.   Since the first apes climbed
down from their primordial trees, human beings have sought
relief from the humble hangnail and so when Dr. Vernon Brilliant walked into a local newspaper office to announce a cure,
there was more than mild interest. When asked for supporting
studies, documentation and peer reviews, Dr. Brilliant is long
on explanations and short on paper. Can reporters cover un-
supported medical breakthroughs?

*Situation 9: The luncheon bill that was mistaken for a con-
tract.*   After meeting for lunch at LaDeduction, Sedgewick
the developer told a reporter for a local TV station that he

hoped their conversation would result in a story. So the reporter would not forget, Sedgewick made a point of having his secretary call the station each day to remind the reporter of their conversation. When, after six weeks, no story was aired Sedgewick wrote a bombastic letter to the broadcaster, which included a copy of the luncheon bill. Was the reporter pleased by such attention?

Situation 10: The obligatory orientation.   Reporter Franklin was compiling a chart of two-bedroom condominium units in the area. He called each of 200 projects, explained what he was doing and asked three simple questions: Do you have two-bedroom units, are any now available and how are they priced? At the "Shacks of Swampmead," the agent told Franklin she would be happy to give the information he sought, but only if he visited the model homes and watched a two-hour video presentation. Guess why the chart was titled "Selected Metro Condos" and the "Shacks of Swampmead" was somehow missing?

C H A P T E R

3

Who Should Do Your Media Marketing?

Media marketing has become a major business with academic degrees, professional associations, high-priced specialists and a level of sophistication rivaling such studies as marketing and business administration. Yet despite the professionalism that marks its best practitioners, media marketing is not a closed vocation with a jealous priesthood holding back knowledge. With study, observation and common sense, most of us can successfully adopt media marketing concepts for our own use and thereby gain the benefits of media coverage.

But which is the better choice? Should you do it yourself or hire a professional? There are arguments on both sides of the question.

Check the yellow pages (under "public relations counselors") and you can find vast numbers of people and organizations providing every possible media marketing service. But how do you select from such lengthy lists? What criteria are appropriate?

Selecting a media marketing professional is much like choosing a lawyer, doctor or accountant. There is more to consider than simple measures such as years in the business or academic degrees. Media marketing is a creative endeavor where chemistry and rapport are important and where no single provider, no matter how able, is right for every client.

The critical measure in media marketing is performance, the ability to create positive distinctions, work well with clients and execute programs within budgetary constraints. Private practitioners and firms of every size can be competitive in a field where ideas take precedence over hardware, square footage and lengthy employee rosters.

Media marketing is more art than science and the ability to generate constructive, usable ideas is crucial. Being creative does not necessarily require the expenditure of vast sums of money, nor is a big budget in itself a substitute for creativity.

Consumer groups, with few promotional dollars, are often masters at promotion even though they may have limited financial resources. Beware of media marketing counselors who suggest spending the equivalent of $81,000 to open a hot-dog stand when you might do better by simply giving out free samples.

Regardless of your project, there are certain basic issues to consider when looking for media marketing services:

Is the individual or firm inventive?   There's no shortage of dull promoters, so find people with a demonstrated ability to create distinction and dimension. When you look at their work, is it clever? Credible? Something that parallels your needs?

Is the firm or individual interested in what you're doing? Some professionals specialize in given fields, such as financial services or retail sales, and they may not have experience with political candidates, product development or whatever.

Is your account of sufficient size to maintain the firm's interest?   If not, do you want to be a small account with a big company, or is it better to be a large account with a small firm or individual practitioner? Realistically, do you have a choice? In the real world it takes a certain number of dollars to justify projects with larger firms.

Is a Media Background Important?

Although many individuals and firms without press or broadcast experience offer excellent media marketing services, it is hard to imagine how hands-on media experience is not advantageous. Former journalists know—or should know—how their business works and how to place stories. Conversely, media experience by itself does not ensure coverage. A past reporter may know a lot about journalism but very little about promotion. Also, his or her experience may be too focused; that is, a client may need help with newspapers, but a former reporter may have only TV experience, or vice versa. The bottom line: If the choice is between two otherwise equal professionals, media experience is a definite edge.

Is the firm or individual so overwhelmed by current clients that their ability to take on new work is limited? In such an environment, it's tough to be creative and give the level of service clients should expect.

Does the firm or individual now serve clients with whom you compete? Practitioners will not normally take on competing clients because of the potential for conflict. For instance, if two construction companies are clients and the practitioner has one dandy promotional concept, which company gets it? Which firm is called if a journalist wants a single interview?

Who will do the work? With large firms, work—such as graphics, typesetting, writing and media relations—is likely to be handled by in-house staff. With an individual or small firm, part of a project will probably be contracted out to specialists. Neither approach is universally better, or worse, than the other.

What about related experience? If a practitioner has done promotion in your field, that can be a plus for two reasons. First, the experienced individual probably has established contacts with media outlets that are important to your program. Second, you don't have to educate him or her about your business, someone else already paid for the training.

What should it cost?   Fees for media marketing services are negotiable and practitioners can be hired at an hourly rate, for a specific project or on a monthly retainer that's a credit against services performed. In addition, media marketing experts often receive an override for such expenses as printing, mailing, etc.

Monthly retainer agreements are frequently used but often misunderstood. The problem is that because practitioners are paid each month, clients feel there should be a major monthly activity. Too often the demand for monthly performance leads to shallow promotional efforts that only devalue a client's overall program. A better approach is to review performance quarterly or by the project.

How can I choose among competing professionals?   Media marketing specialists meet prospective clients through personal contacts, advertising and sometimes even through media coverage. Once a contact is made, the client usually receives a proposal explaining what the firm or individual will do, how it will be done, how long it will take and what it will cost.

Proposals, however, cannot be too specific. If prospective clients receive an in-depth analysis of their communication problems plus a point-by-point series of solutions, complete with wording, artwork and documentation, then the media pro's services are unnecessary. Pros try to offer a fine balance, suggesting how they would approach a problem without giving the client enough material to do it alone.

From your perspective, if someone can't take the time to write a decent proposal, or if they can't communicate their ideas well, it's wise to seek alternative assistance.

Can I get guaranteed results?   Beware of promoters who promise the world ("Sure, work with us and you'll be right on the cover of *Time*"). Ethical, rational professionals can only promise to make a credible effort, to use their skills fully and to work in good faith. They want your business and to do less would be foolish; to promise more would be ridiculous.

THE CASE FOR DOING IT YOURSELF

One of the most attractive aspects of media marketing is its democratic nature. While there are many pros in the field, there's always room for newcomers with fresh ideas. You don't need a license, there's no entrance fee and media marketing is not restricted to those with advanced degrees or 20 years of training.

Another attraction is price. It can be far less expensive to go the do-it-yourself route than to hire a professional. However, "less expensive" does not mean "free." You need to consider the value of your time and the fact that it's likely to take a lot longer for you to do the things professionals quickly accomplish.

If you're a physician and earn $100 an hour, paying $50 for an established pro can be a bargain. If you make $5 an hour, hiring someone else may not be an option.

Can you do it? Many promoters can, and many promoters have, especially individuals and those involved with small organizations.

There's no better way to receive a media marketing education than to go out and devise your own promotional package, prepare materials, contact reporters and see what happens. But if going solo seems too hard or inconvenient, then try a mixed approach: Do some of the work yourself and hire a professional for the rest. You can pay by the hour for consulting or pay for a specific set of services. In either case, be certain to have a written agreement showing exactly what is expected, compensation, when payment is due, if there will be an override for expenses and how disputes will be resolved. The last item, resolving disputes, may seem unimportant, but it is much easier to build in a binding arbitration clause when a relationship first starts than it is to work out a quarrel when everyone is angry.

You can obtain help in many areas, from creating strategies to writing news releases, and if some portion of your program is too technical or difficult, the pro is there to do the work. A mixed approach offers something to both the promoter and the pro. You gain access to professional services as you need them. The pro acquires an opportunity to work with you, demonstrate skills and get paid. Presumably, as your program grows, so will opportunities for the professional.

C H A P T E R

4

Successful News Releases

The most important period in the media marketing process is when programs and strategies are first developed. Getting in print and on the air may be both profitable and productive, but the odds of getting media coverage are limited unless journalism's five basic questions can be answered.

Media marketing programs evolve because we all have self-interest. Our desires may include more sales, higher profits, greater recognition or whatever, goals we can often enhance through positive media coverage.

Journalists, however, have a different perspective. Their interest is not in how promoters benefit, but how readers, viewers and listeners are aided by a given story. To test the validity of a story idea, to see if something or someone is newsworthy, reporters will ask five basic questions the public will want answered: Who's involved, what happened, where it took place, when it occurred and why. Here's how these questions might be discussed if a new bank opens in town.

Who is involved? By "who" we mean an identifiable interest or entity such as a company, civic organization, governmental agency or individual. "Who" can also be a collective interest such as consumers, employees, clients or people down the block. Sometimes a "who" by itself can guarantee story interest if the "who" is a movie star, congressman or the hometown kid who became a success.

Knowing who's involved and who's affected tells you which publics need to be reached. The bank opening may interest business readers, local residents concerned about traffic, publications that follow the industry nationally, people who want to find discount checking, and nearby residents looking for work.

What is the story about?   With the bank opening there may be a major theme (bank to open) as well as several minor story ideas such as a company history, growth in the banking industry in general, local banks versus big city rivals, how the bank may bring other businesses to town, etc.

Where did, or will, the story occur?   The answer is significant because people relate to one another on the basis of location. We root for the home team, read about our neighbors, listen to area politicians and watch local weather reports. News outlets, in turn, often gear their stories to location. The community newspaper, by definition, will exclude matters that do not affect the neighborhood. The local radio station tells us about commuter tie-ups in our area, but not distant cities. The local paper will write about the bank opening, but not about a bank that opens in Norway.

When did, or will, the story occur?   News is time-sensitive and with the bank opening we have several deadlines. The official opening will be arranged with newspaper and television deadlines in mind. If the local paper has a 3:30 P.M. deadline, the opening ceremonies may be held at 10 A.M.—an hour chosen to allow reporters enough time to attend the event and finish their stories well before any deadlines.

The bank opening lends itself to less time-sensitive feature treatments as well. There are pre-opening stories ("Bank Seeks New Workers"), post-opening stories ("New Bank To Have Biggest Vault in Town"), and follow-up stories ("One Year Later: New Bank Deposits up by $50 Million"). These stories have a time sequence; if one isn't used today, it can be published or aired tomorrow with little problem.

Why is the story important? The answer to this gives reporters an opportunity to evaluate a story concept. Our bank opening may interest the public because it's a local story or because a new bank suggests an expanding economy and more future jobs. If the bank uses new forms of automation, then the story might be intriguing because some people refuse to use automatic tellers and other mechanical devices.

It seems reasonable to believe that if journalists can have their questions, promoters are entitled to a few of their own: For instance, how much time, energy and money are you willing to expend on promotional activities? Is there any way publicity can hurt you? Will competitors, for example, be able to see news coverage and discover trade secrets? What happens if your promotional efforts fail?

What is most notable about promotional planning is how often initial presumptions and approaches are tossed out when viewed through the questions journalists will ask. What happens is not that self-interest is eliminated, but that self-interest is channeled into productive directions. Here are several examples:

- An association wanted its members included under federal insurance legislation and wanted the media to support its position. But why, it was asked, should members be included? A variety of answers followed, almost all of which fell in the category of self-interest. When people began to think how patients could benefit, an entirely different set of ideas emerged and a far more salable program evolved.
- A group of medical professionals was offered the opportunity to automate its office with equipment that could greatly speed patient evaluations. The technology was terrific and once installed it could lead to considerable local news coverage. But despite these advantages, the high-tech route was ultimately rejected. Why? Because the machine's very efficiency was a problem. Speedy exams would produce higher patient volumes, but less time to talk with patients. And talking with patients, personal communication,

was a more valued quality to these practitioners than
speed, money or their names in print.

• A major corporation wanted an institutional brochure to
  discuss company products, plants and services. But what
  made this company different from competitors who also
  had nice products, big plants and offered similar services?
  What differences would interest prospective clients? It took
  two weeks to outline definable answers, but the company
  found a far stronger identity and produced an effective
  brochure as a result.

MISUNDERSTOOD RELEASES

Journalism has its five standard questions and promoters
have a standard response: the basic news release. Although a
news release should be seen as *nothing more than a brief communication alerting reporters to a possible story*, the concept
has grown to the point where news releases are today shrouded
in mythology, misunderstanding and mystique.

News releases are misunderstood because lurking between
the visible words one can often find a host of unwritten as-
sumptions. It's these expectations, rather than material in the
releases themselves, that often sour relationships between journalists and promoters.

False Assumption 1: News releases equal news.   News releases
may sometimes be news, but in all circumstances they're tools
designed to influence media coverage. The mere existence of a
news release does not ensure that it's accurate, in context, factual or complete. The central problem here is that we would
each like to define how we are seen by the world and so a news
release reflects our self-perceptions. News, however, requires a
range of perspectives rather than just a promoter's solitary
viewpoint.

*False Assumption 2: A news release is successful when it's
aired or printed verbatim.*   If one has a limited sense of
"victory," then perhaps getting a release printed or aired is a

success of sorts. The difficulty is this: If a publication or station uses your material verbatim, how credible is the rest of their *news?* If credibility is limited, how valuable is the victory?

Suppose a news release says, "Colossal Industries earned $2.3 billion in the last year." Could a journalist just air or reprint this statement on faith in a news story?

To use this release verbatim assumes it's true and, in effect, that the journalist believes it's true. But even if the material is correct, it still could not be used in its present form. The problem is attribution.

If the statement from Colossal Industries is used verbatim, a reader, listener or viewer will believe the words are those of a reporter. This difficulty can be easily resolved by saying "Colossal Industries reported sales of $2.3 billion in the last year." Now we at least know it's the company claiming sales and not the reporter attesting to the firm's figures.

It's possible to have news releases printed verbatim when they provide for attribution or when their content is largely "data" as in names, dates, places, etc. A release announcing a new 27th vice president might qualify.

False Assumption 3: A news release is successful when the information it contains is used by reporters. Yes...and no. It's surely a good sign when release information appears in the media, but this is not the pinnacle of success. There is a higher standard by which releases should be measured: Is the release so interesting reporters call back to build their own stories?

The idea of media marketing, after all, is not only to obtain coverage, but to receive as much coverage as possible. If a news release sets in motion a series of events that lead to a feature article or lengthy interview, that's a far bigger success than just having a paragraph or two buried in a major publication or used for five seconds in the midst of a lengthy broadcast.

False Assumption 4: News releases are useful because they allow promoters to spread material quickly to a large number of iournalists. It's true that news releases can be used to disseminate information widely and with speed. But is this good? Not always.

If 25 reporters receive the same release, the information is hardly exclusive, and some journalists may not bother with the story precisely because of its broad distribution. Newsletters, for example, will hesitate to use information if they feel a general circulation publication has the same material.

False assumption 5: All news releases are meant for the media. Some portion of the huge number of news releases received by the media are never intended for publication or broadcast. They are, instead, the products of internal politics, releases sent out because someone with ego (and clout) needs to be mollified or because an itchy client wants *action*. Rather than argue, it's easier to write a release, send it out and then if nothing comes of it, blame reporters. ("Well, we're trying sir. Just last week we sent out 14 releases, all with your name right there in the very first paragraph, but for some reason we just can't get past those hacks in the media. But don't worry, I've checked the supply room and we've got 41 cases of stationery on hand, enough to churn out 50 or 60 releases a month for the next six years.")

False assumption 6: Journalists can't wait to read the next news release. Maybe it's the movies or television dramas, but somehow the idea has developed that reporters eagerly arise each day yearning for the latest consignment of releases.

Think about it. Do you enjoy getting mail from people you've never met? Are you thrilled by the prospect of receiving 15 unusable pieces of mail each day? Will your level of delight rise or fall if the number reaches 100 or 200 unwanted releases per day? How will you feel about such a daily influx after six months on the job?

The problem for journalists is that buried within each day's literature may be the seeds of a worthwhile story, so looking through news releases is a necessary chore. And because the mail must be read—or at least skimmed—promoters have a chance to compete for a reporter's time and attention. That opportunity makes the development of a workable release worthwhile.

NEWS RELEASE BASICS

If you shuffle through 100 news releases, the probability is that they will each have an essential similarity. This likeness stems from the idea that with news releases, as with good architecture, form must follow function.

The purpose of a news release is to quickly convey information in a competitive environment. Although placement, positioning and utility "sell" the release, a release will be incomplete, if not useless, without certain resource information.

What is resource information and why do you need it?

Go back to the idea of a successful release. A winning release is not merely a handout used verbatim by the media; rather, it's a device designed to stimulate editorial coverage. If a release is complete, if it contains all the quotes, concepts and ideas anyone, anywhere, will ever want, a journalist has little incentive to look further or to ask questions.

A release that's more than a basic announcement ("Fred Wilson Named Manager") should entice reporters. One sure way to encourage inquiries is to produce a delicately balanced release, one that tells enough of a story to generate interest, but not as much as a journalist might want to know.

Since a good release is incomplete, it must say where reporters can find more information. It's these details that comprise the "resource" material found in every good release.

Resource information may seem dull, uninspired and uninspiring but like a good timetable it has its uses. Here's what you need:

Who sent the release?   The individual's name and organization (if any) plus an address should be shown, usually by a logo or in a single-spaced, typewritten block in the upper left-hand corner of the page.

Inspect-All Industries   Contact: Lyle Jones
Kemp Mill Industrial Park   703-555-1800 (Office)
Zongrass, NM 80234   703-555-1820 (Fax)
                                                    703-555-0987 (Home)

FOR IMMEDIATE RELEASE:

STRUCTURAL INSPECTIONS MORE COMMON

Forty percent of all first-time home buyers now use a structural inspector according a nationwide study conducted by Inspect-All Industries.

"Buyers want more assurance in the marketplace," says Ralph Woolsley, Inspect-All's president. "They want to make certain that the dream of a lifetime is not a nightmare of hidden flaws."

The survey found that 52 percent of all sellers or seller agents suggested the use of an independent inspector because, said Woolsley, they wished to limit the possibility of future claims and litigation.

Not all buyers sought inspections, however. The three most common reasons against inspections cited by purchasers were cost (22 percent), satisfaction with the property (18 percent) and cost-free alternatives (20 percent) such as examination by a relative.

Inspect-All Industries is the nation's largest source of test kits, forms, probes and water detection devices for residential inspectors. Approximately 50 percent of all inspectors involve the use of company equipment or services.

- 30 -

Is there a contact? A name and phone number should be at the page top, usually in the upper right-hand corner. Some media relations firms favor naming both the client and the promoter while others list only the client but use the promoter's name. Either approach is acceptable.

Is there an embargo date? Sometimes news is "embargoed"; in other words, a release time has been established for it and broadcast or publication is prohibited prior to that time. Embargoes may be established with a capitalized banner above the body of the release stating: "NOT FOR RELEASE PRIOR TO APRIL 30TH AT 10 A.M. EST."

Embargoes make sense in only the most limited situations. For instance, a magazine may send out a release about a hot new story a week before the latest issue hits the stand. Early distribution may be required to reach media nationwide but advance publication would hurt sales; therefore the publisher establishes a release date and time.

But embargoes should be avoided for several reasons: They may be ignored, they're a barrier to coverage (there's enough news available without waiting for someone's carefully timed release) and a specific release time may hurt some outlets and favor others (morning versus afternoon papers, for example).

A suggestion: Skip fancy embargoes. Just write in capital letters above the copy, "FOR IMMEDIATE RELEASE," and everyone will be happy.

Do you need a headline? News releases often contain a brief headline to identify the promotion's subject and angle.

For whom is the release written? If the copy is single-spaced, it's fairly useless to a reporter or editor because there's no room for editing marks or additions. Always double-space material.

Is it a novel or a blurb? A release should be short; one page is best. If the release must be two pages, use two separate sheets of paper. That way if the material is cut apart by reporters who want to use certain paragraphs, material on the back of the page won't be lost.

How To End It All

It's a journalistic tradition to put "- 30 -" at the bottom of news releases (and news copy) because, as the story goes, the first telegraph message was 30 words long. To end the transmission, the telegrapher wrote "30" so the receiver would know how many words were in the message. It's quaint, but it works.

SUPPORTING EVIDENCE

To some degree the process of attracting media attention can be compared to a multi-stage rocket; each stage has a particular function, but place the stages in the wrong order and the rocket becomes unworkable. A news release can be seen as the first stage in a promoter's effort to gain media interest, but what works well in stage one is often inappropriate later.

No matter how well-written, informative or interesting, a proper news release is a physically brief document and thus, by definition, its contents are limited. And although the notion of being to the point bodes well when initially competing for a reporter's time and attention, it can also be something of a liability further along in the story selection process.

For journalists, the first efforts to screen story ideas often involve rummaging through bales of letters, releases and phone messages. In this environment brevity is important.

But in the second go-round, when only plausible story ideas are being considered, conditions change. While there are fewer competitors, the competition that remains is far tougher. All the releases and letters say something of interest to the reporter, but not all will result in coverage.

Releases in the second go-round wash out for a variety of reasons. Some are simply less significant than others. Some are victims of poor timing, a condition that often arises for reasons well beyond the promoter's control, such as a heavy news day or conflicting journalistic schedules.

But many releases are unusable for a curious reason: They don't provide supporting documentation. In effect, the brevity that made them attractive in the first sorting causes them to fail in the second.

The solution is to recognize that if you want coverage then something more than a basic news release is typically required. Rather than a news release, a *news package* is needed, a package that includes both a release and supporting materials to substantiate claims and validate ideas. The news release gets the promoter through the first sorting while the supporting materials—longer, more detailed information—clarify issues in the second go-round.

The case for supporting materials and information can be demonstrated in three common situations.

Suppose the reporter is a generalist. He or she may receive 30 wildly different story ideas in a day. Since no one can possibly be an expert in so many fields, it's important to have supporting information to document a story idea.

Alternatively, the reporter may be a specialist, in which case he or she may be an authority in a given area. It's unlikely that a news release will contain enough detail to satisfy a reporter's interest and so more information will be needed.

The third case simply reflects common sense. Journalists are busy people. If they have a choice of two equally valid story concepts and one requires ten hours of research and the other three hours, which story will be pursued?

There are an endless variety of additions that one could plausibly include with a news release. Here, with admittedly elastic definitions, are the most common and useful items to include.

Fact sheets. In essence a fact sheet is often nothing more than a stark news release, a listing of basic information. For example, if the Tick & Tock Clock Company has just developed a new wristwatch, one that plays Top 40 hits, a news release might discuss the watch and what makes it unique. A fact sheet could describe the company and its size, production facilities, annual sales, work force, other products and industry rank or market share. A second fact sheet (yes, there can be more than one) might look at the watch's technology, how its production is automated and how new songs are added each week.

Question-and-answer sheets.   Q&A sheets are effective because they allow promoters to first frame and then answer selected questions. The information is presented in a format that's easy to absorb and a wide range of subjects can be covered.

Histories.   Capsule histories are particularly useful, since they provide background and show the relationship between the subject and a given industry, idea, community, etc.

Documents.   If your mailing list is either short or selective, it can pay to send entire documents such as reports, studies and even books. If you send a document, it also pays to mail a brief summary. Anyone who then wants to read the entire document will have it available for study.

Photos.   Pictures can supplement a news release if they're black and white, $8'' \times 10''$ glossies for newspapers or 35 mm color slides for magazines. Check with local TV stations for individual requirements.

Videotapes and audiocassettes.   Often developed by professional producers, tapes and cassettes can be very useful, particularly for electronic media. Beware: Long tapes and cassettes are unlikely to hold someone's interest. Go for three to five minutes of pithy material.

Although supporting materials may be costly to assemble and produce, yet they should never be sent out on a widespread basis with the expectation that they'll be returned. Think about it this way: If a candy company gets your name from a mailing list and unilaterally sends you a box of their latest concoctions, are you required to send it back?

NEWS RELEASES THAT FAIL

Although the idea of a news release is to generate media attention, the huge proportion of unused releases suggests something is wrong; somehow even promoters who know the mechanical requirements for good releases (names, phone numbers, double spacing, release dates, etc.) are offtrack.

How is it possible to create a news release that's unusable even though the subject is potentially newsworthy? Botched news releases, unfortunately, are easy to concoct, particularly when the promoter doesn't understand why a release is imperfect.

Failed release 1: The CEO who cried "wolf." " 'Federal lawmakers will have to ease tax restrictions on domestic feldspar production if industry capacity is to rise,' according to Homer T. Smith, president of the Obscure Minerals Council."

On its own this release is OK. The difficulty is this: Homer has denuded an entire forest knocking out daily releases for the past five years. Editors receiving envelopes from Homer don't open them because Homer is just not important enough to be a daily news feature. The tragedy for Homer is that every so often he says something that deserves coverage.

Failed release 2: Translation, please. "At a recent convention of all major mechanical testing associations, Lazlo T. Hunzindonger, executive director of the National Coalition for Micrometer Reform, announced that an independent standards review committee, which will have a major impact on mechanical testing, has been established and is now in effect."

For all the information it conveys, this release may as well be written in a particularly obscure Babylonian dialect. What's the point? Why will the new committee make a difference? From whom or what is it independent? When is "recent?"

Failed release 3: What company was that? "Fromqualf Industries announces the introduction of the Fromqualf QUADRAPOWER LASER REAMER, a remarkable improvement on the Fromqualf DYNOPOWER LASER REAMER. The new Fromqualf QUADRAPOWER LASER REAMER will use LASER POWER to vaporize as many as FOUR olive pits SIMULTANEOUSLY, thereby increasing productivity in this KEY FOOD PROCESSING AREA."

The difficulty here is that Fromqualf has produced nearly unreadable copy because its name is used repeatedly and far too many words are capitalized. Why not rewrite the same information in plain, uncapitalized English and drop a few "Fromqualfs."

Failed release 4: The miraculous, the wondrous, the overblown. "The greatest event in computer history will occur today when King Arthur Computers introduces the amazing, wondrous, labor-saving Round Table #111, a computer that will revolutionize the entire computer industry if not the Western World...."

Journalists are constantly bombarded with new idea and product announcements, many hawked in terms that would embarrass P.T. Barnum, were he alive. Reporters tend to view such claims with skepticism, in part because a single day may bring in three "wonders," six "miracles," 14 "marvels" and at least one "awesome."

Failed release 5: Too much, too soon. It's 9 A.M. sharp when a delivery truck pulls up with what looks like a carton of lead pipes. But wait! It's not building materials, it's merely a single news release of Olympic proportions; a 26-pounder. Can it be that a reporter will devote an entire day—or week—to reading this massive document? Is it true that the entire release is single-spaced? Can it be there is no cover letter, summary or index? Does anyone believe reporters will use such releases for anything other than door jambs, pressing flowers or ballast?

Failed release 6: For the lack of a proofreader... "The Central Club will feature Govenor Hern Simth as its guest speaker on...." If a release is full of errors, particularly names— *Governor Henry Smith* in this example—journalists may wonder about the credibility of both the release and its promoter. A release should be read by at least three people or checked with a computer spelling program before it's mailed.

WINNING COVERAGE WITH NEWS RELEASES

Given the various myths, requirements and pitfalls involved, it's little wonder that most news releases fail to generate much attention. Developing a one-page document that tells an interesting story is tough, but the toughest part of all is compressing and encapsulating ideas, concepts and values into two or three introductory sentences.

Decisions to read or dump a release are undoubtedly made in the few seconds it takes to scan the first sentences. If something in those 50 to 100 words doesn't capture the reader, forget it. The rest of the release won't be read (why bother?), nor will fact sheets, histories or anything else.

It's clear that most releases fail in the first few words because the wrong points are stressed. Suppose the average family spends $600 a year on gasoline for cars and suppose further that a company has patented a new carburetor that increases gas mileage by 20 percent. This is an important invention with enormous consequences and yet, so often a release will begin, "Charles Magrew, president of Wesnack Industries, announced today..."

Is Mr. Magrew the subject of the release? As a promoter, do you want your fortunes to depend on a Magrew quote?

Winning news releases address two crucial questions upfront: What's the point and who's interested? The significant issue above is not that Mr. Magrew is quotable or that his firm has a new invention, but how readers, viewers and listeners will benefit. How much better to say:

> Cars across the country will soon deliver higher gas mileage than in the past because of a newly patented carburetor that cuts fuel usage by 20 percent. The new device is expected to lower family gasoline costs by $120 a year while dramatically reducing U.S. dependence on foreign oil.

Now we have a release that makes several points in 50 words: Gasoline consumption can be cut with a new invention. Families will save money. Our country will be better off. If you were a reporter (or stockbroker), wouldn't you want to know more?

News Release Checklist

Releases that lack energy, focus and purpose are common. They reflect the abilities of their authors, devalue their subjects and represent a gross waste of paper, postage and time. Before sending out a release, ask five basic questions:

1. Does the release get to the main point immediately?
2. Does the release use quotes appropriately?
3. Does the release provide a suitable platform for backup materials?
4. Is the release as short as possible, hopefully no more than a single page in length?
5. Does the release include all necessary resource information such as contact names, phone numbers and addresses?

So now we have an enticing lead. Much has been promised. Let's back it up.

A patent for a new fuel-efficient carburetor has been granted to Wesnack Industries of Wesnack, Md. The device employs an advanced chamber design that causes fuel to burn more completely. Testing over a two-year period under federal supervision showed gas savings of 14 to 31 percent, with typical users cutting consumption by 20 percent.

From the second paragraph it's easy to see how supporting materials can be developed. What will help reporters?

- A summary of test results? Absolutely.
- A copy of the patent? It's more theater than information but it does make the point that a patent was granted, that there is legitimacy to the product.
- The carburetor's history? Go back to the first carburetors and show how they evolved.
- A photo or diagram showing the difference between a typical carburetor chamber and the new design? Yes.

- A background feature on the company? Absolutely. Let's find out who these bright people are.

So now we've created a worthwhile lead and given it some supporting information. What about a human dimension? We could just add another paragraph, but if we put the same information in the form of a quotation from the company president, we may earn more coverage.

Reporters are not hired to reprint releases verbatim but there is one major exception: Quotations. A quote can be clipped from a release and used directly in a story because it's attributable to the speaker. Therefore, if any part of the release is to survive the newsmaking process intact, it's likely to be a quote.

Knowing how quotes can be used, knowing that the rules for quotes and general prose are different, a promoter can package a release so that certain points are likely to be emphasized in news accounts.

"We believe the Wesnack carburetor will cut the average family's $600 annual gasoline bill by $120," said Wesnack President Charles Magrew. "In total, the widespread use of this new device should reduce foreign oil imports by 1.5 million barrels a day within five years, a savings to our country of $16.2 billion a year. With less demand, we may see further savings as a result of generally lower oil prices."

Here we've turned from the company and its technology back to family savings and national benefits. A study of consumer gasoline purchases would be a valuable supporting document here as would a question-and-answer sheet discussing U.S. oil imports.

We could close at this point but there's a little more room at the bottom of the page and so another sentence or two is in order. How about a quick cost/benefit analysis:

Wesnack predicts that its new product can be installed for $110, a price that typical families will recover through lower gas costs within a year. A Wesnack carburetor used for five years should save a typical family $490 at today's gasoline costs.

Wesnack Industries   Contact: Bill Smith
225 West Main Street   301-555-7000 (Work)
Wesnack, MD 20902   301-555-7045 (Fax)
                                          301-555-3984 (Home)

FOR IMMEDIATE RELEASE:

NEW DEVICE PRODUCES LOWER GAS COSTS

Cars across the country will soon deliver higher gas mileage
than in the past because of a newly patented carburetor that
cuts fuel usage by 20 percent. The new device is expected to
lower family gasoline costs by $120 a year while dramatically
reducing U.S. dependence on foreign oil.

A patent for a new fuel-efficient carburetor has been
granted to Wesnack Industries of Wesnack, Md. The device
employs an advanced chamber design that causes fuel to burn
more completely. Testing over a two-year period under federal
supervision showed gas savings of 14 to 31 percent, with typical users cutting consumption by 20 percent.

"We believe the Wesnack carburetor will cut the average
family's $600 annual gasoline bill by $120," said Wesnack
President Charles Magrew. "In total, the widespread use of
this new device should reduce foreign oil imports by 1.5 million barrels a day within five years, a savings to our country of
$16.2 billion a year. With less demand, we may see further sav-
ings as a result of generally lower oil prices."

Wesnack predicts that its new product can be installed for
$110, a price that typical families will recover through lower
gas costs within a year. A Wesnack carburetor used for five
years should save a typical family $490 at today's gasoline
costs.

- 30 -

If you were a reporter, what stories would you see here? Think of the possibilities: How will this device effect local gasoline sales? Who will install it? Can I buy one today and if not, when? How will this development affect local service stations, car dealers and consumers in the area?

A well-written release creates interest, inspires questions and starts a dialogue with the media. If a release doesn't do these things, save a tree, save postage and save a reporter the time it takes to toss out still another unusable release.

A NEWS RELEASE ALTERNATIVE

There's little doubt that the simple news release is the single most common form of promotion. Releases are so common it's tough to write one that stands out, but even if someone creates an interesting release, one has to ask: Is a news release the best way to reach the media?

We live in an increasingly streamlined society, one that's computerized, refined, purified and in too many cases sterilized as well. News releases are part of our modern era, a form of mass communication that allows us to reach many reporters quickly and with minimal effort. In a word, news releases are efficient.

Is efficiency appropriate? Are there situations where being efficient is not the best strategy?

Our ability to move information quickly from one location to another thousands of miles away is remarkable, particularly in the historical context of entire centuries being dominated by messengers, drums, smoke and—who knows—maybe carrier pigeons. Yet although the *means* of communication have been vastly altered by technology, the process of *creating* information remains an art. At some point, a live person must develop a concept, write the words and produce the graphics that make modern communication worthwhile.

There is a fundamental conflict here. Journalists create customized work in an era of mass production. And promoters, for the most part, send standardized materials to journalists—

a practice that's the equivalent of mailing a paint-by-numbers kit to a fine artist.

The point is not that news releases should be banned (although there is a substantial body of opinion within the journalism community that would probably support such an idea), but rather that instances exist where the use of mass-produced news releases are inappropriate and unproductive.

Why is it wrong to sit down and write a letter to a reporter explaining why a story is worth covering? Since individual media outlets serve different audiences and typically offer a vast array of perspectives, why can't promoters originate separate, customized letters for different journalists, letters that show why a particular subject will interest that reporter's specific readers, listeners or viewers?

Writing individual letters is a time-consuming and expensive proposition, one that greatly resembles work. But it offers benefits that should not be overlooked.

In an era emphasizing mass communication, individual contact stands out. A letter writer is not only someone who is literate, but also someone who has invested time, thought and energy to communicate with a specific individual. In response, a journalist is likely to invest his or her time reading such missives, if only because they're so rare.

Although writing individualized letters to journalists is attractive, many promoters are tempted to skip personalization and head for the nearest computer keyboard. Why not meld mailing lists with word-processing wizardry to produce computer-generated correspondence? With a good word-processing program and a letter-quality printer, one can produce individualized letters all day that are correctly spelled, devoid of typos and prepared by devices that do not tire, smoke, go out for lunch or strike. Just as important, properly prepared letters are indistinguishable from those written on word processors or electronic typewriters.

Computerized mailings, when properly done, offer the possibility of personalized letters without the drudgery of manual labor. Yet while computerized mailings are not a bad idea in theory, in practice something is often lost. Who among us has not received a "personalized" letter saying:

Dear Mr. Resident:

Yes, MR. RESIDENT, we are sending this personal letter directly to you, MR. RESIDENT, because we know that green, healthy lawns are an important part of your life-style. Certainly you want the RESIDENT property to be the best-kept yard on the block and so we at Plague's Lawn Service are now offering for a limited time only a tested, ten-point program...

Writers of letters similar to the above missive apparently believe that form letters can be magically converted into personal correspondence through the repeated use of a recipient's name. Nobody wrote to Mr. Resident individually; his name just popped up on a mailing list, perhaps because he lives in a certain ZIP code, subscribes to a particular magazine or belongs to a given association. Surely recipients will wonder about the credibility of the letter writer's product, service or idea if the letter itself is nothing more than a heavy-handed, outright sham.

In like fashion, letters to reporters often abuse computer technology. It's tempting to lean back, press a button and send out 200 identical letters. But when TV correspondents get letters explaining how a story will benefit "readers," or city magazines are peppered with identically worded letters to eight staffers, it's obvious that button-pressers are at work.

Using computers to generate personal letters may seem like a contradiction, but properly employed, computers are nothing more than glorified, labor-saving typewriters. A well-written letter is a well-written letter, whether it's produced with a computer or an almost-prehistoric manual typewriter.

The use of computers should be restricted to the mechanical aspects of letter writing such as typing and data. "Data" includes names, addresses, dates, salutations and return envelopes—all of which can be prepared mechanically without sacrificing individuality.

As alluring as computerization may appear, the sight of whirling daisy wheels and spinning diskettes should cause promoters to keep their goals in mind. The ultimate purpose of letter writing is not to save time, but to gain coverage. If the choice is between mailing 100 computer-generated letters that

Computer No-No's

Although computers can greatly speed the letter writing process, it's important to avoid an assembly-line look. Here are several tips:

- Do not use form paper that tears at the edges. The tears are visible or can be felt. Either feed individual pages into a letter-quality printer by hand or buy an automatic sheet-feeder.
- Do not use a dot matrix printer.
- Do not justify right-hand margins. For a hundred years typewriters have produced ragged right margins and so should computer users, if only to enhance the sense of individual preparation.
- Do not type a name and address onto a preprinted form and expect the results to pass for personalized correspondence. Invariably the individual characters don't quite match or the colors are somewhat different.
- Type envelopes and letters on the same machine.
- Never use italic or Old English type for correspondence unless you're determined to produce an unreadable document.
- Always use stamps when mailing personalized letters. Postage machines represent efficiency in a situation where stamps, and the effort and inconvenience of attaching them to a letter, suggest individual labor and attention.

look as if they came off an assembly line, or mailing one letter written with a quill pen, practice your penmanship.

There's no reason why a personalized letter cannot include a news release and background materials. Indeed, individualized cover letters will greatly enhance the value of such standardized materials precisely because they customize appeals.

As with news releases generally, no one guarantees that writing letters to journalists will result in coverage. But if you were a reporter, which will stand out more: Another cookie-cutter, look-alike news release or a letter from someone who made an effort to understand your audience and your needs?

C H A P T E R

5

Contacting the Media

There's no shortage of possible media targets to write or call. A promoter with enough time and money could probably find several hundred thousand potential contacts, but the names and addresses valid at one moment would undoubtedly be out of date the next. Media contacts are always in flux and while no one knows how many news releases are sent each year to people who changed jobs, retired or died, the postal bills and telephone tabs for such errant messages could probably underwrite much of the national debt.

For promoters the sheer number of media outlets is a major problem. You want up-to-date names and information, but you don't want to spend 12,000 hours compiling lists. Conversely, you can't have an effective media marketing program if you don't know who to contact.

Fortunately there are many directories and guides that track the media. Here's a list of particularly useful references, including several usually found in local libraries.

Bacon's Publicity Checker ($195). Published yearly with quarterly updates, this two-volume set lists more than 17,000 publications and 175,000 editorial contacts. Bacon also publishes *Media Alerts* ($195 including bimonthly updates), a directory of 1,700 magazine editorial calendars and a *Radio/TV*

Directory Suggestions

When considering the use of different publications or services, readers should keep several ideas in mind.

First, as the lawyers say, prices, addresses, phone numbers, content and availability are subject to change. Also note that many publishers have several prices for an individual item. There might be one cost if an order is prepaid and a second and higher cost if the publisher ships first and bills later.

Second, the use of directories for particular purposes may be restricted. It's easy to understand, for example, that publishers wouldn't want someone to merely copy their materials and then produce a competing volume. If you have any question regarding the use of a directory, check first with the publisher.

Third, if you need mailing labels, many publishers make them available. An often better choice is to get a directory on a computer disk arranged so that it can be entered into a data base management program. If you buy a disk be sure you understand any restrictions imposed by the seller. For example, if you are buying a license to use the information, how long does the license last?

Fourth, if you're buying a directory in the state where it's produced, ask about the sales tax.

Fifth, if you're calling an 800 number in the state where the publisher is located, you may need a statewide 800 number or a local phone number rather than the national 800 number found in this book. Check telephone information for details.

Directory ($195 including quarterly updates), which provides listings for network and local news and talk shows, PBS stations and college radio outlets. Another Bacon product, the *International Publicity Checker* ($210) provides expansive contact lists for 15 countries in Western Europe. All are available from Bacon's PR and Media Information Systems, 332 S. Michigan Avenue, Chicago, IL 60604 (800-621-0561; In Illinois, call 312-922-2400).

Broadcasting Yearbook ($95). A massive compilation of electronic broadcast media, this reference includes listings for radio (AM and FM), TV and cable outlets as well as a history of broadcasting, FCC rules and regulations plus information about producers and distributors. Broadcasting Publications, Inc., 1705 DeSales Street, N.W., Washington, DC 20036 (202-659-2340).

CPB Public Broadcasting Directory ($12). Published annually, this reference work lists all public radio and television stations by state along with an extensive personnel list at each outlet. Also includes a listing of non-station organizations with interests in public broadcasting. Write to Finance Office, Corporation for Public Broadcasting, 901 E Street, N.W., Washington, DC 20004. Note that prepayment is required.

Editor & Publisher International Yearbook ($80). An authoritative directory of U.S., Canadian and foreign newspapers. Also contains census data and separate sections for African-American, religious, ethnic and university papers. Editor & Publisher, 11 West 19th Street, New York, NY 10011 (212-675-4380).

Gale Directory of Publications ($265). This excellent three-volume compendium includes approximately 22,500 media outlets arranged by location and contains daily, weekly and twice-weekly newspapers, magazines, journals and newsletters. Also includes TV and radio outlets. Gale Research, 835 Penobscot Building, Detroit, MI 48226 (800-877-4253).

Gebbie's All in One ($73). A single directory with 22,000 listings for daily and weekly newspapers, radio and TV stations, general/consumer magazines, business papers, trade publications, African-American press, farm publications and news syndicates. Also has computer disks and labels available. Gebbie's Press, P.O. Box 1000, New Paltz, NY 12561 (914-255-7560).

Media News Keys ($125). A quarterly update that goes into a loose-leaf binder and shows media personnel information for radio, TV, magazines and newspapers in 35 to 40 top markets (some markets, such as Dallas-Ft. Worth, San Francisco-Oakland and Minneapolis-St. Paul, are combined). Media News Keys, 40-29 27th St., Long Island City, NY 11101 (718-937-3990).

Capital Connections

By any standard Washington is the nation's media center and there are at least three solid guides to the capital press corps.

First, the *Congressional Directory* contains a listing of reporters accredited with the press galleries of the House and Senate. Here you can find newspaper, magazine, radio, TV and photo journalists. Published by the federal government, this publication is available in virtually all libraries as well as through Government Printing Office bookstores. ($15 in paperback, $20 in hardcover.)

Second, many of those who write and broadcast in the capital area do so on a free-lance basis. Washington Independent Writers is an association of free-lancers that includes many experienced, well-connected journalists. The group's membership directory ($15) lists members by name and also cross-indexes by specialty. Washington Independent Writers, 220 Woodward Building, 733 15th Street, N.W., Washington, DC 20005 (202-347-4973).

Third, *Hudson's Washington News Media* ($119) is a comprehensive listing of the Washington press corps that includes nearly 5,000 reporters. Purchase price includes three quarterly updates. From Hudson's Directory, P.O. Box 311, Rhinebeck, NY 12572 (914-876-2081).

Hudson's Newsletter Directory ($99). A useful and well-organized publication that lists subscription newsletters by subject category, this directory shows addresses, phone numbers, frequency of publication, cost, year founded as well as the names of editors and publishers. Just as important, each publication is coded so that directory readers can tell if the letter will consider press releases on industry news, personnel changes, financial news, product news or photos. In addition, the yearbook also lists publishers with three or more newsletters (in which case you can often cut down your mailing volume) and publishers by location. The Newsletter Clearinghouse, P.O. Box 311, Rhinebeck, NY 12572 (914-876-2081).

Oxbridge Directory of Newsletters ($245). This directory contains information concerning approximately 18,000 subscription and non-subscription newsletters. Shows names, addresses, phone numbers, etc. Oxbridge Communications, Inc., 150 Fifth Avenue, New York, NY 10011 (212–741–0231).

Publication Mastheads. The most direct method to update media contacts is to check publication mastheads and broadcast credits. In addition to core staff, look for contributing editors and regional staffers who may be more accessible than high-ranking reporters in far-away central offices.

Talk Show Selects ($185). A listing of nearly 650 radio talk show hosts, producers and programming executives with station call letters, addresses and phone numbers. Available in a bound edition (280 pages in 1991) and on index cards, floppy disks, and press-on labels. Broadcast Interview Source, 2233 Wisconsin Avenue, N.W., Washington, DC 20007 (800–955–0311).

Working Press of the Nation ($295). A five-volume reference series that originated more than 40 years ago, *WPN* includes personnel listings, deadlines and material acceptance information. The newspaper directory (Volume 1) has more than 60,000 personnel entries, while the magazine directory (Volume 2) includes trade, professional, farm and industrial publications. Volume 3 is a TV and radio directory with listings that include more than 25,000 local radio programs. Freelance writers and photographers are featured in Volume 4 and internal publications produced by various corporations and associations are found in Volume 5. Note that Volumes 1 through 3 are priced together at $265, and individual volumes can be ordered for $140 each. National Research Bureau, 225 West Wacker Drive (Suite 2275), Chicago, IL 60606 (800–456–4555)

HOW TO PHONE REPORTERS

In seminars and articles around the country, the latest buzzword in promotion is "telemarketing," a concept with an undeniable logic: If everyone has a phone then the phone system can be used to reach every home and business. And it follows that if every reporter has a phone, every promoter can call.

In theory, there's nothing wrong with one individual calling reporters. In reality, two major problems arise. First, *one* promoter never calls, dozens phone and part of a reporter's day is lost as a result. Second, journalists must answer their phones because otherwise they may miss important stories. Conversely, few calls lead to prize-winning articles or broadcasts.

Calling reporters, then, represents an opportunity for promoters. But like news releases, too often calling is both overdone and self-defeating.

It's not that calling reporters is offensive per se, but rather that cold calling is uniquely invasive. If a promoter sends a news release to a newspaper, the release can be read or scanned when time is available. If the phone rings, however, an immediate response is required. Whatever work is in progress will be interrupted and when reporters are in the midst of developing stories or writing broadcast materials, such interruptions are tough to justify.

Magnifying the irritation quotient is the oft-transparent nature of such calls.

Hello, Mr. West. We're wondering if you got our news release last week.

Hello. When do you think *Nimrod's Journal of Wrestling,* the authoritative monthly review of gore, culture and fine interstate dining establishments, will run more features on rope manufacturers? You know, if it weren't for the ropes, American wrestling might look just like sumo matches.

Hello, Ms. Kelly. Just wanted to see if you got the case of melons we sent along with that release on 400 summer recipes.

Worse yet, some phone efforts are less organized than Napoleon's retreat. What can you say when a reporter is called nine times in a month by a single promoter or six times in two days ("Are you sure you're not going to write about the new aquarium at Phil's barbershop?")?

Phones make reporters *too* accessible and therefore they need to be used with caution. Promoters have a limited goodwill allowance and no one benefits if it's spent on needless or offensive phone calls. Phoning, then, should be seen as a possible method of communication, but only within limited circumstances.

Promoters should never call, for example, to confirm the arrival or use of a cookie-cutter news release sent to 400 reporters. If a reporter isn't important enough in the eyes of a promoter to receive an individualized letter, then the promoter has not invested enough time or interest to justify a phone call.

But if you have written an individualized letter, if you are contacting just three or four reporters before sending out a news package or if one reporter is crucial to your program, then calling may be acceptable.

The call should be brief. If you want local real estate coverage for a new townhouse development, your end of the conversation might sound like this:

> Ms. Conners? Yes. My name is Mr. Whitman and I have a quick question. We've just started to market earth-covered townhouses over at Sundale and we wonder if you would want us to send information about what we're doing.
>
> We've been active in town for 12 years and we think that with our new energy-efficient product and unique architecture we'll grow substantially in the coming year.

If the reporter is interested, the response will probably be something along the lines of, "Send the information. I can't promise we'll do the story, but let's see what you've got."

You can now send a cover letter ("When we spoke by phone this morning...") with your release and background materials.

Note that in the call above *the reporter was never asked if she would write about townhouses*, just if she was interested in receiving more information. Asking a journalist if he or she will write about a given topic is the equivalent of obligating the reporter to do the story. Since a writer or broadcaster may not have enough information to make an immediate decision, and since reporters are constantly pushed to make commitments, the answer is likely to be "no." There are too many stories with less hassle that can be pursued.

Should You Fax?

One of the great wonders of modern business is the humble fax machine, a device that has made immediacy both possible and inexpensive.

There are people out there who fax news releases, sometimes with extensive back-up materials attached. Faxing releases to large numbers of reporters is certain to antagonize many people, if only because it ties up their equipment and uses their paper.

If sending a general release by fax is not a good idea, then what is? A fax can be used appropriately in several ways.

First, if a reporter requests information, a fax is OK.

Second, if a release is being developed and a reporter wants a copy as soon as it is available, a fax is fine.

Third, if your release is going to reporters you know, faxing may be acceptable. A better approach is to ask the reporter if he or she wants the material mailed or faxed.

Fourth, if you do fax make certain you fax correctly. Few reporters have individual fax devices. Since equipment is typically shared, a proper cover sheet showing the recipient's name and the number of sheets being sent is required.

Fifth, if something is confidential, don't fax. Use the mail, a delivery service, or see the reporter in person. A fax transmission should never be regarded as private.

Note also that a brief phone conversation is the oral equivalent of the first few lines of a news release. Know what you're going to say before calling because there's a premium for being brief and to the point. Can you describe in 60 seconds why your story idea will be interesting to readers, listeners or viewers? How about 30 seconds?

You have a few seconds, literally, to stimulate interest so it's appropriate in such circumstances to write out your pitch, practice till you get it right, and then call. Never read a pitch over the phone. Fair or unfair, journalists often evaluate public contacts quickly, in part because they receive so many.

There seem to be several protocols to observe if you're going to call reporters,

First, avoid deadlines. If a reporter has to finish a story by noon, don't call at 11:30.

Second, never use an automatic dialer with a taped message to contact a journalist (or any other human being).

Third, always return calls.

Fourth, don't call at the beginning of the day (9 A.M. sharp) or at the end (4:51 P.M.). People need their psychic space, some time to get organized, settled and adjusted. Calling in the midst of this process is unsettling.

Fifth, leave messages. If a secretary or machine answers the phone, say who you are, why you're calling, where you can be reached and when.

Sixth, be brief. Socialization makes it hard to hang up on people but many reporters have overcome this handicap and will put down the phone if a caller's point is not immediately clear.

Seventh, leave both work and home numbers when contacting reporters. The newspaper you read December 26th must have been written Christmas day and to produce that paper it's inevitable some people were called at home. Reporters, particularly those employed by daily newspapers and electronic outlets, often work weekends, nights and holidays, which means access to sources is needed at those times.

Eighth, don't phone repeatedly after the first call or letter. Reporters know you're out there.

Ninth, if you're calling long-distance, don't phone collect. Phoning a reporter is a business deal and the cost of phoning is just one cost of doing business. Note that many news organizations have 800 numbers.

Tenth, if for some reason you have an automated phone answering system ("Press 5 to reach the order department, press 9 to hear today's lumber prices, etc."), make a point of leaving a number that will be answered either by yourself or another sentient being.

Some who read these opinions may feel compelled to disagree and if so, that's fine. But please, if you want to make your sentiments known—just write.

PROMOTIONAL HELPERS

The overwhelming majority of all promotions are local affairs where the potential number of contacts is limited. Even in a major metropolitan area, promoters may only find 50 or 100 relevant contacts, a manageable number.

What happens if you have a bigger project, one involving ten cities or a broad array of media outlets? Suppose you're faced with hundreds or even thousands of outlets. The physical process of gathering names and preparing materials will consume enormous amounts of time and money.

One shortcut is to rent mailing lists from directory publishers or from mailing list brokers (found in the yellow pages under "mailing lists"). "Renting" is not the same as "buying" and users should be careful to understand the distinction. When you rent or license a list you normally have the right to use it one time, or for a limited time. To prevent unauthorized reuse, lists are sometimes salted with house names that ultimately go back to the list owner. If the list owner gets several mailings from one rental, there's written, dated evidence that at the very least more rent is due.

Lists are not always available to prospective purchasers. In the mailing list game, you not only need money, you sometimes need prior approval from a list owner or broker as well. If you want to reach all redheaded, left-handed taxidermists, there may be such a list. The catch is that if the list has been compiled by an organization that views you as a competitor, they are unlikely to rent out their cherished names for just a few cents apiece.

List rentals are normally based on a cost per 1,000 names, say $50 or $75 per 1,000 labels, and lists may be developed by states, regions, cities, selected ZIP codes, income, employment, credit card use, car ownership or thousands of other criteria.

An alternative to self-mailings is to use a specialized service that takes your release, develops a distribution list and then sends out the materials. One major service, Media Distribution Services, maintains lists of more than 150,000 writers, editors and broadcasters at more than 40,000 outlets. These lists, in turn, have been divided into more than 2,500 categories. (Contact: Media Distribution Services, 307 West 36th Street, New York, NY 10018, 212-279-4800.)

If you want to reach Capitol Hill and the Washington press corps, consider the Chittenden Press Service. For $75, 450 releases you supply can be delivered to media outlets in the National Press Building, in the Capitol Hill press galleries and other locations. Chittenden also has a congressional messenger service that will hand-deliver releases to receptionists in all congressional offices, a service Chittenden says is faster—and cheaper—than mailing. Chittenden Press Service, 1277 National Press Building, Washington, DC 20045 (202-737-4434)

In addition to mail or hand delivery, several services will now take news releases and other documents and send them electronically to media offices where connections are located.

Electronic services are attractive because they eliminate paper, postage, envelopes, labels and mail delays. In a matter of minutes your fresh, time-sensitive, hot-off-the-wire materials can be in newsrooms around the country.

Newswires are electronically connected to newspapers, news bureaus, magazines, local TV and radio stations, network newsrooms and business publications. In addition to newsrooms, some services are also tied into investment and research departments at major brokerage houses, pension funds and various data bases. Information may be sent nationwide or to given regions and areas. Firms offering electronic services include Business Wire (1185 6th Avenue, New York, NY 10036, 800-221-2462) and the PR Newswire (150 E. 58th Street, New York, NY 10155, 800-832-5522).

Another approach to news distribution is offered by the North American Precis Syndicate, an organization that sends materials to the nation's suburban publications, which, says NAPS, represent 94 percent of all newspapers and publish more than 100,000 pages a week.

What NAPS sends out is a weekly booklet with 20 or so stories in a camera-ready format complete with columns, headlines and artwork. Such materials may produce from 100 to 400 clippings as well as orders, mail to Congress and other benefits. NAPS also packages materials for radio and television.

NAPS, 1025 Vermont Avenue, N.W., Washington, DC 20005 (202-347-7300).

With so much material being sent to the media you may wonder if any of it actually gets printed or aired. To answer this question there are clipping services and Burrelle's is believed to be the largest. Burrelle's says it covers nearly 1,900 daily and Sunday papers, 8,000 weeklies, 6,000 magazines as well as radio and TV stations in most major markets as well as all broadcast networks. For prices and coverage contact Burrelle's at 75 East Northfield Rd., Livingston, NJ 07039 (800-631-1160).

HOW THE MEDIA CAN FIND YOU

If you think about it logically, it figures that if directories can help promoters find media contacts, then there should be resources to help reporters locate promoters. There are at least three sources reporters use to find story ideas and promoters.

The *Yearbook of Experts, Authorities & Spokespersons* ($38.50), for example, is a fascinating 800-page guide that is distributed to more than 5,000 journalists. If a producer wants to put together a show on gun control, for example, organizations for (Handgun Control, Inc.) and against (Citizens Committee for the Right to Keep and Bear Arms) are listed, with names, addresses and phone numbers.

For promoters the beauty of the yearbook is that you can be listed just by purchasing an ad. For information, contact the Broadcast Interview Source, 2233 Wisconsin Avenue, N.W., Washington, DC 20007 (800-955-0311).

If you've ever heard a radio announcer pep up your day with an unusual—but real—anniversary or celebration, the information probably came from *Chase's Annual Events* ($32.45). If you're preparing a special day or week, this is the place to be announced, a famous guide where your event may appear in the 30,000 copies printed each year. No charge if your listing is published, but send information no later than May 31st to make the following year's issue. Mail details about your day (or week or month) plus names, groups (if any), addresses, contacts and phone numbers to Chase's Annual Events, c/o Contemporary Books, 180 North Michigan Avenue, Chicago, IL 60601 (312–782–9181).

Newsmaker Interviews is a monthly subscription service distributed to 138 radio stations nationwide as well as newspapers, television outlets and free-lance writers. Forty-five people and organizations are covered each month in 200-word capsule reports. No charge if you're profiled. Provides subscribers with information, access and contacts to many newsmakers, including leading personalities in the Hollywood community. ($40 per month base subscription price.) Contact: Arthur Levine, President, Newsmaker Interviews, 8217 Beverly Blvd., Los Angeles, CA 90048 (213–655–2793).

The publications above are obviously good targets for promoters because they're able to successfully gather information of interest to the media. Considering their cost, currency, purpose and audience, they represent an enticing opportunity to reach numerous media outlets without travel or travail.

HOW TO CREATE A SUCCESSFUL NEWS CONFERENCE

"Ladies and gentlemen, the President of the United States."

With those words begins one of our most visible and intriguing American institutions, a presidential news conference, one spectacle certain to dominate the day's events.

Presidential news conferences set a standard that cannot be matched. With the White House as a forum and reporters vying for both seats and presidential recognition, what promoter doesn't envy a president's power to attract news coverage? How wonderful to set a time, preempt television schedules and know that members of the fourth estate will fill the room.

From a promoter's perspective, news conferences offer the possibility of dealing with large numbers of reporters at a single time and in a single place. That's efficient, cost effective and far better than trying to schedule interviews all over town.

But developing a successful news conference isn't easy. It requires all the preparation and thinking needed to build a winning news package, and more.

To start, one has to announce the conference with either a cover letter, news release or formal invitation complete with RSVP notation. With the announcement comes an information package—news releases, question-and-answer sheets, histories, photos, fact sheets, etc. These items define the story, give it perspective and provide background information.

Another way to announce a news conference is over the local "day book" or schedule of events run by news wires in larger cities. To list a news conference, call the local office for AP or UPI, ask how a news conference should be listed, and see how much advance notice is required.

Creating an effective news package is tough—we already know that most news releases fail to produce much coverage—and asking reporters to attend a news conference is even harder. Since news conferences are so difficult to organize, promoters should ask if one is even necessary before sending out the first invitations.

Why call a conference? Is the subject so important that reporters will interrupt their schedules to attend? It's difficult enough to interest journalists in news releases and with a news conference, you're asking them to travel back and forth, attend the event and then consider doing a story. The news value has to be so plain, so obvious, that your invitation doesn't fly right into the dumper with the daily crop of unusable releases.

Is there a time element that makes a news conference necessary? News conferences tend to work well with breaking stories —an important announcement or a new development. A story that can wait until tomorrow or next week is likely to get more coverage through individual interviews.

What will reporters learn from a news conference that they can't pull from a news release or individual interview? Good reasons include the demonstration of a new product or technique, the opportunity to question someone who usually isn't in town or a conference to examine a complex event, such as a report, study or trial.

On the Record or Off the Record

Virtually all information given to journalists should be regarded as "on the record," an expression that means a reporter can use the material you provide without restriction and cite you as a source.

In some situations, however, information may not be on the record.

Information provided "off the record" is material reporters can't use directly in their stories. Such information may provide leads for journalists, and in this sense off-the-record material may have value. A journalist may be able to get the same information from another source, especially if he or she knows where to look.

"Background" information consists of material a reporter may use or quote but without identifying the source. When you read that a "senior adviser to the President" said something, you're reading the fruits of a background interview.

Most reporters avoid anything other than on-the-record interviews if possible. Should it happen that you want to provide information on an off-the-record or background basis, be absolutely certain before giving the interview that both you and the reporter agree how the material is to be handled.

For a news conference to be successful it must be not only newsworthy, but also convenient, properly timed, good theater and carefully prepared.

Convenience.   The central purpose of a news conference is to attract media attention not otherwise available through a simple news package, and so it follows that a conference should be arranged to meet the media's needs rather than those of the promoter.

To start, you need a reasonably central spot such as a local press club, downtown hotel, private restaurant facility, corporate boardroom or country club. Less pedestrian choices include off-shore oil rigs, airplanes, laboratories, airfields and yachts. Note that if your conference must be held at an inconvenient location, such as a factory far from town, it pays to charter a bus or limo to transport reporters from a central location.

Wherever the conference is scheduled it must offer certain amenities. TV crews and news photographers, in particular, often have special needs.

Make sure, for example, that your conference site has adequate electricity. At one Washington news conference a past vice president walked into the room, strong lights from half a dozen television crews went on and every fuse in the place blew. The Secret Service was understandably concerned as the entire room went dark.

Other items to check at a news conference include background lighting (never have a window behind a speaker), handicapped access, sound systems (set microphone levels prior to the conference), film or slide projectors (keep spare bulbs handy and make certain slides are in the correct sequence and right side up) and background noise (beware of locations near ambulance routes, civil defense sirens and new construction).

Timing.   Different media outlets have different deadlines and so it follows that promoters will want to schedule conferences to benefit as many media timetables as possible. Many conferences are scheduled for 10:30 in the morning, an hour that's attractive because it works well for most outlets and also offers a natural endpoint: Lunch.

Presentation.   A news conference can be the ultimate show-and-tell performance, an opportunity to take advantage of good visuals, demonstrations, test runs and strong speaking skills. It's OK to offer news and a little "theater," as long as the presentation is responsible, in context and appropriate.

For instance, when a small railroad wanted to demonstrate a new automated switching system it didn't just show a room full of computer consoles. The company took reporters from a downtown terminal by private railroad car, through its yards and then to the switching center. The 100-year-old car was a unique setting for interviews and a stark contrast to the firm's modernization program. Was the car ride necessary? No. Did it make for a better story? Absolutely. Did it attract reporters? Sure, wouldn't you want to spend a day riding a private railcar?

Preparation.   Some promoters believe news conferences should be spontaneous events where speakers just wing answers. This is a gutsy approach, but one totally lacking in common sense. A far better strategy is to set up mock conferences beforehand where speakers are grilled and answers perfected in a less meaningful environment.

Absentees.   Be sure to send materials designed for distribution at the conference to those reporters who couldn't attend, along with a transcript of questions and answers raised at the meeting.

THE CASE AGAINST NEWS CONFERENCES

Although news conferences seem to be an attractive ploy to draw media interest, in the real world they're often unsuccessful. Check the news desks in any major city and it's probable that dozens of full-blown news conferences are being scheduled every week. It's equally probable that many, if not most, conferences don't draw vast hordes of reporters or produce much coverage.

What's wrong with news conferences? How come they often fail?

The basic problem with news conferences is that many are inappropriate and some actually bar media coverage.

At first it may be difficult to see how a news conference could reduce the impact of a given story, but conferences, by their nature, raise subtle problems.

Journalists are intensely competitive and there's a clear preference for exclusivity and being first. But a news conference is a group affair; there is no exclusivity and everyone gets the same information at the same time. That may be convenient and cost effective for promoters, but it's not so enticing to reporters.

The idea of a news conference presumes that with adequate notice journalists will arrive at the appointed place and at the proper hour. This presumption exists in a vacuum because promoters can't know what breaking events may conflict with their conference or whether competing—and possibly more interesting—conferences are scheduled for the same time.

One attraction of news releases is that such media calls as may result can be handled on an individual basis. If you flub a reporter's question there's usually some give and take, some possibility of correction or amplification. Just as important, a weak answer with one journalist will not damage interviews with other reporters. They'll have separate questions and if the same difficult matter arises again, perhaps the question can be handled more adroitly the second time around.

With a news conference there's a wholly different environment. Questions beget questions, sometimes because reporters like to demonstrate their knowledge in front of competitors (and sometimes in front of TV cameras). Rather than being a one-on-one, human-to-human interchange, a news conference is more formal, more institutionalized. There's less margin for error and if a question isn't handled well, it won't be a private matter.

Because news conferences are usually a public affair, packaging stories for individual media outlets is tough. There's no way to keep competing reporters from hearing the same information, or seen from the reverse perspective, there's no way to divide a story into separate parts that can be used by different journalists.

As for utility, news conferences group journalists together regardless of individual requirements. The magazine reporter and the radio broadcaster (assuming both come) share the same information at the same moment, despite their vastly different professional requirements. Production needs guarantee the broadcaster will produce the story first.

Simply stated, news conferences are inappropriate for many topics and events that might otherwise receive media attention.

The opening of an insurance office, for instance, is unlikely to warrant a full-blown briefing, but if the broker can offer information of value to the media, there may be a story. But whatever story there is, if any, it's probably best developed by meeting one-on-one with reporters.

CHAPTER

6

Electronic Media

Although there is always room for the daily paper and other forms of print media, modern America is decidedly influenced by radio and television. From breaking news stories to election night results, nothing has more impact or immediacy than the electronic media.

From a promoter's perspective, the best news about the electronic media is that each year they seem to be increasingly accessible. Today a metropolitan area is likely to have four full-blown network outlets (CBS, ABC, NBC and Fox), numerous independents, public television, 30 or 40 cable options, and a growing number of all-talk radio stations.

Given this vast array of opportunities, appearing on radio and television should be regarded as neither mysterious nor implausible. Simply stated, the number of stations, programs and outlets is now so great that anyone with an interesting subject and a good stage presence should be able to find airtime. Here's how.

RADIO

With more than 10,000 radio stations throughout the country, it's not surprising that radio talk-show hosts and producers are eternally looking for guests to capture audience minds, hearts and ratings—preferably at the expense of other stations. Indeed, given competitive demands and vast amounts of time to fill, it's easy to argue that of all the media, radio presents the most opportunities for coverage.

Getting on radio talk shows is a straightforward process: Call the station, ask how guests are booked and then send out individualized letters to each booker with a news release and background materials.

What should the letter say? It should identify you and your credentials, but more importantly, it should package an idea in terms that will interest a given audience.

For example, psychology is a talk show staple and a social worker might suggest a program discussing "interpersonal relationships among family members at holiday times."

Ugh!

Real people don't use such convoluted language, but the topic has potential. Why not repackage it in terms that can generate greater interest?

Dear Ms. Host:

When the family gets together at Thanksgiving is something wrong? Do you find that time spent with Uncle Ned or Aunt Fran is less enjoyable than it should be?

Many people feel this way because family gatherings are often not what they seem. Genealogy may be shared, but not necessarily interests, life-styles or values. There's pressure to compete (Does younger cousin Willy make more than you?), pressure to perform (Still not married?), anxiety (Have you gotten a new job yet?) and often embarrassment as well (Remember when George was a teenager...).

As an experienced social worker with an extensive private practice, I'd like to talk about how to take the sting out of family gatherings, how to make them less tense and more enjoyable. It's a topic that affects everyone and I'm certain your listeners would be greatly interested. Tell me what you think.

The mere fact that you've sent a coherent package of materials to a station should create interest. What usually happens next is that someone from the station, such as a host or producer, calls to find out more about you and your subject. They'll listen to your answers and try to gauge your guest potential. Do you answer questions without a lot of rhetorical mush? Do you use jargon? Can you explain complex ideas in a simple manner? Do you use examples that relate to listeners?

In effect, the conversation is an audition and if you "pass" you'll get booked.

Before appearing on a show it pays to turn on the program for several days and hear how the host deals with guests. Is the conversation friendly? Abusive? Do listeners call in? How much airtime does each guest receive? Are there many interruptions for commercials, news breaks and traffic reports? What topics does the host seem to favor? Breaking news? Features? Fluff?

Once on the air you'll discover that radio is an especially wonderful medium because, unlike good children, guests are heard but not seen. There's an opportunity to "appear" in public and yet still preserve one's privacy. No one cares what you wear or how you look.

Usually you'll wind up sharing a table in a small room with a host, and in this setting it's okay to bring papers and books and spread them out for reference. A caution: Some stations allow smoking and coffee in studios, others don't. Ask what the policy is. A second caution: Don't move microphones or make noise. Radio equipment is sensitive and tapping the table or touching a microphone creates sounds that can be picked up.

A common radio format is the call-in show where John and Mary Public have a chance to air their views. The host serves as kind of a moderator between the guest and the listeners, introducing the topic and then taking calls.

Most stations check callers before they're allowed on the air, merely to see if the questions are relevant. When callers are not screened, however, questions from out of left field are entirely possible: You're discussing fall fashions and the caller wants to know if the stock market will rise by spring.

Do Your Own Show

Rather than vie for a guest spot on someone else's show, some promoters have turned to a relatively new option, the radio advertorial. Buy a block of space, say 30 minutes, and you get to have your own show. The station provides a studio and an engineer and from that point forward you're in command. You can have guests, call-ins and commentaries and if you do it right, you might even find a sponsor.

A radio advertorial mixed in with music programs or talk shows can be an effective marketing tool. Beware, however, of saturation, a situation that can occur when a station has sold most of its airtime to promoters. Where programming is uneven and clearly self-serving, ratings are likely to be weak.

Call-in shows are great for promoters because they allow immediate interaction with the public. You raise an idea, listeners respond. They raise an idea, you respond. The questions themselves can be seen as kind of a community opinion poll, one that's admittedly skewed by frequent callers and zealots, but a poll which nevertheless gives some idea of what people think. After doing a few call-in shows, you can sense listener interests just from questions and comments.

From the listener's perspective, call-in shows are attractive not only because they allow participation, but because callers participate anonymously. While guests are identified, callers named "Don of Closter" or "Mary from San Ramon" can be anyone.

Calls need to be handled diplomatically. Disagreement is okay, berating listeners is not. One good tactic is to reverse roles and question listeners; this gives callers a platform to explain their ideas more fully. Knowing about health, real estate or politics is fine; being too specific can raise problems. For instance, how do you handle these questions:

My friend and I have a nifty idea to beat the IRS. We're each going to buy cars, set up car rental businesses and then rent to each other at bargain rates. This way we can get all sorts of tax advantages, just like a business. Ain't this great?

If you agree, you may be in the position of endorsing a sham arrangement or outright fraud. The best response, if taxes are your field, is to explain that the goal of a business is to produce profits and refer the caller to a CPA or tax attorney.

Isn't it true that the democrats (or republicans or whigs or whoever) lied about taxes last year?

This is an assertion posed as a question. The caller wants your agreement, not your opinion. Once you answer, whatever you answer, the caller will then say, "Yes, but isn't it true..." After one or two "Yes, buts" you'll need to change callers or the show will stall. "OK, obviously you have an opinion, why don't we see what other listeners think?"

Could you predict interest rates for next June?

Being a talk show guest makes you an authority figure and some listeners therefore feel you should know everything. Sometimes it's best to handle speculative questions with humor, to say for instance that, "I've been predicting interest rates for more than 20 years and in all that time I've never been wrong. Basically, I believe interest rates will change. Whether they go up or down is a different issue."

Your success as a radio guest will depend largely on how well you interact with the host. Recognize that it's the host's show, his or her territory, audience and format. Most hosts are intelligent and personable, friendly people, and you'll get along well with most of them if you're merely prepared and straightforward.

Some hosts, however, will not win contests for congeniality or charm. There are the "sharks" who regard guests the same way wild dogs view raw meat. Regardless of your ideas or positions they'll roast you on the air. More deadly still are the "chameleons," hosts who are delightful off the air but instantaneously turn into snarling interrogators once the mikes go on. After a warm conversation before the show, you may wonder if the host has a twin elsewhere in the building.

The "common man" is another type of host. Rather than preparing questions about you or your subject, the host simply engages in conversation. This can work well when the host is broadly knowledgeable, but if the host rarely reads you could be in for a long interview.

If you do well in radio there's often a bonus: You stay on longer. Hosts will frequently say "we've scheduled you for an hour but if we get a lot of calls, could you stay longer?" Translation: "I'll let you hang around if you pep up my audience."

Because radio is an oral medium it's entirely possible to do live shows away from the station. If you're a successful guest, a host may suggest (or you might propose) future programs by telephone. So-called "phoners" or "phone feeds" allow you to do shows in distant cities without leaving home, a great way to save time and travel costs.

It's tough to arrange phone feeds if you haven't been on a program or station at least once, but there are several ways to raise the idea.

Certainly it pays to write to hosts and producers in distant cities. Not only do you want to describe your topic and yourself, you also want to mention your radio experience ("As a frequent guest on many radio programs, I thought...."). In addition to your letter, you'll want to include a news release, background materials and perhaps an audiotape as well. Rather than just a tape of yourself, send a copy of an actual show. It's realistic and proves you have experience. Before sending copies, however, make sure you have written permission from a host or producer to use the material.

Another approach is to call a host or producer. There are many stations and you could run up a huge phone bill calling each one, but a less expensive strategy is to find stations and programs listed in toll-free, 800 directories. Phone and ask for a copy of the broadcast schedule and staff roster, wait a few days, and then call back and ask for a specific host or producer.

In timing calls, don't phone while a show is on the air (people are busy), just before a show (the program is being planned

---

Phone Feed Etiquette

Doing phone feeds on a regular basis is easy to arrange, especially for those promoters who are prepared. Some suggestions include:

- Never use a speaker phone. The sound quality is often poor and listeners will hear if Rover barks in the next room.
- Consider a good quality headset instead of a handset. A headset frees your hands while talking, a decided advantage. Headsets also prevent "telephone arm," a condition that can arise when on the phone too long.
- In an office setting, have the radio station call a separate number rather than a line with 14 extensions. A direct line will eliminate the problem of unwanted interruptions.
- If you work from home, have the family out of the house or suitably quiet while you're on the air.
- Never do a feed with a phone that can be interrupted with a call-waiting "service" or any other distraction.

---

and finalized) or immediately after a program leaves the air (hosts and producers usually need some time for themselves). Try an hour before a program or 15 to 30 minutes after a show ends. If someone isn't available, ask when it's convenient to call back.

TELEVISION

Millions of Americans spend a large portion of their day before television screens, and so it's little wonder that TV has such influence and power. Yet for television to be successful, if we define *successful* as high ratings and growing ad revenues, then TV producers must continually find new and interesting stories, personalities and information or face the prospect of losing both viewers and their jobs.

How I Got on Oprah

The Oprah Winfrey Show is a television icon, a program seen by 15 to 20 million people a day. Given such numbers, getting on a show hosted by Oprah or Phil Donahue is the promotional equivalent of a home run, touchdown and three-point basket—all on the same day.

How did I wind up on Oprah? The answer tells a lot about the way media operates.

A reporter for *USA Today* wrote a story that appeared on the paper's front page. It was a great story about a new form of home financing and when a producer for Oprah called the writer to get more information, she suggested a call to one of her sources: Me.

For a period of several weeks the producer and I spoke regularly about buying a first home and then one day he asked if I would like to visit Chicago and be on the show. And so it happened on July 4, 1990, that I spent a full hour on national television in front of one of the largest audiences available to any promoter.

P.S.: About that story in *USA Today*. I was never mentioned in the front-page piece that appeared. I was merely a good source, proof that being a good source sometimes can be valuable.

The search for something interesting to televise is compounded by television's staggering ability to consume information and entertainment. All of Shakespeare's plays, the work of a lifetime, are just a few nights' viewing. Scheherazade, who kept her husband entertained for 1,001 nights, would have been exhausted by television in a matter of weeks.

Talk shows and news programs are typical targets for promoters. As with radio, you need to check directories and call stations to see who does the booking, most probably people identified as producers, assistant producers, production assistants, talent coordinators, assignment editors or news directors.

TV bookers have no shortage of "talking heads," people who can sit and discuss events, news or whatever. Guests with good visual presentations, however, are in demand.

Part of the trick to obtaining TV coverage, then, is to offer something visual. Riding a llama, exercising on a mat or trying out a new product all serve to enliven television. If you can take what you do, give it a visual twist, your chances of TV coverage will be greatly enhanced.

Whatever visual presentation you make must not only illustrate your subject, it must also be brief and workable. On a TV talk show with several guests, you're likely to have eight minutes of airtime to yourself—or less. Visuals must be quick and to the point, so it pays to practice demonstrations before going on the air. Another tactic is to prepare part of the demonstration before the show and begin in midstream. ("Well Mary Jo, as you can see we've already got the button weaver started and now we'll show you how to turn those ugly household knick-knacks into beautiful buttons anyone in the family can wear.")

Ah, but what if you're not going to make the evening news and you don't have a visual presentation? What if you are a talking head, a couch person; can you get TV coverage?

Talk shows are filled with people who sit, speak and do little else. Their attraction is in the words they use, the way they appear and their ideas, opinions and insights. They are, dressed up and polished, the very same people you would want to hear on radio. After all, would you be interested in someone who could help you save money or lose weight? Would you listen to someone who just conducted a poll on the ten biggest battles in marriage or the five best dates?

TV talk shows favor those with visual presentations, but several of the most successful syndicated programs on television feature little more than one or two guests, questions from a host and audience participation. These programs succeed because they ingeniously package subjects in formats that create public interest.

If, as a promoter, you can develop a good talk-show package—a focused topic with a unique approach plus several hot guests—your chances of appearing are excellent.

Cable Affairs

When considering television appearances promoters should not overlook cable programming. Not only does cable reach millions of homes, but cable consumes so much material that programs are often repeated several times.

Talk show bookers look for guests who are not only qualified to speak on a given subject, but who are also distinguished by a personal dimension, something in their character that comes across in public. One could argue that successful guests should be urbane sophisticates who exude style, grace, charm and charisma, but how often is this true? Some guests—and some hosts—are rude, combative, abusive and yet eminently interesting. They succeed not because they're seen as role models, but because in a mundane world they add spice, zest and vigor.

TELEVISION NEWS

Time on a TV news program is even more precious than it is for a talk show. If you get more than four minutes exclusively, you're lucky. Two minutes is a coup.

For TV news you need visuals and you need something else, the ability to speak in "20-second sound bites." Your ideas, arguments and reasons must be compressed into quick phrases that instantly transmit ideas.

For instance, if you're asked why lower mortgage costs are beneficial, don't launch into a detailed discussion of compound interest or loan amortization schedules. No one cares. Respond in terms viewers can understand. Sometimes the question is best answered like this:

Did you ever wonder why lenders have the biggest buildings in town? It's because borrowers pay too much interest. Instead of paying tens of thousands of dollars in excess interest payments, here's what you can do...

TV assignment editors and assistant producers are always looking for people who communicate ideas quickly and with flourish. You can't use jargon or define 26 exceptions on the nightly news; there isn't enough time and even if there was, you wouldn't get booked.

There's a temptation to think that because TV news appearances are short, they're devoid of content. This viewpoint is grossly in error. Some of the most telling communications of our time succeed precisely because they are short and to the point. If you can create a shorthand phrase, expression or action that immediately and dramatically captures an idea, then you have a powerful selling tool. As an example, when George Bush said "read my lips" on the issue of taxes in the 1988 presidential election, no one had to pore through 80 pages of documentation to understand his position.

For promoters to obtain TV news coverage you need to show a viable news angle and a strong visual component. The news angle can be expressed in a letter, news release and background materials, but developing a visual component often is more complex. Sure, you can suggest scenes from the factory or an office lobby, but in developing a story proposal, remember that programs have few camera crews and their time is extremely limited.

Location and background shots that are close to the station (less travel time) and require little advanced preparation are thus preferred over productions that would awe Hollywood. One business network, for instance, routinely has guests on a nationwide talk show and then interviews them later for news broadcasts. Rather than filming at a distant location, the network finds an empty office in its own building and shoots the interview right there. On TV, the setting looks appropriately professional.

WHAT HAPPENS BEFORE AIRTIME

To succeed on television you need more than good ideas. Presentation is important, but presentation is often difficult

How To Perk Up TV Performances

What can you do to enliven TV coverage? Here are six quick strategies.

- Invite the program to do a "remote" from your site. A remote can range from a few moments of tape introduced on the air ("Here's a brief tour of the O'Dell bakery where the world's largest pretzel is being assembled") to an hour-long program ("We're live today from Wedding World, where we're going to see what's new this year for brides and grooms").
- Have a partner. While you talk, someone else can demonstrate a product, dance, cook, exercise, model or create. Your partner provides the visuals but you remain the authority figure.
- Bring samples. ("Well Tom, just for fun we thought you'd like to have the one billionth Cranston's cupcake. We didn't know which flavor is your favorite, so we boxed 100 different samples, everything from chocolate on chocolate to raisin danish strawberry. We'll let you take your choice and then share the rest with the crew and audience. Incidentally, we've also donated 5,000 packages to the homeless shelter on McGrue street and the Police Boys Club on Carter Hill.")
- Involve the audience. ("Could we have somebody come up here and try these new dripless paint brushes?")
- Involve the host. ("Fred, we thought the best way to test our new triple-action seat belt was to arrange a small demonstration. We've set up a car seat...")
- Use examples. Fill your presentation with illustrations that are short, relevant to the audience and understandable. Ask who watches and then tailor examples appropriately.

because few people, even those who frequently speak in public, are used to the environment of a TV studio.

Suppose you're a guest on the "Bill Local Show." You'll be asked to arrive at the station anywhere from 15 to 45 minutes early, a period used for permissions, introductions, attire, reviews and makeup.

Permissions. Most talk shows and many news programs will want you to sign a permission sheet, a statement that gives the show authority to use your name and image for promotional purposes. Such permission statements often contain language that makes you legally responsible for slanderous statements.

Introductions. When you arrive at a station someone on the show's staff will typically greet you in the lobby and then escort you to a "green room" to wait until airtime. The green-room usually contains newspapers and magazines as well as a large color television so you can monitor whatever is being aired. Here too you can meet other guests. ("Oh, so you're a lawyer defending the civil rights of a gopher. How interesting. And you're on before me...")

Attire. Television is a visual medium and you need a proper wardrobe. Avoid white (it glares on camera) and provocative or unseemly clothes—aside from being inappropriate, they devalue your position as an authority figure. Good dress is commonly equated with good thinking, though obviously there need not be a positive correlation between the two. Test yourself, if two people are talking about gold futures, who are you more likely to believe, someone in conventional attire or someone who shows up wearing a toga and scuba gear?

Reviews. Once in the green room (which rarely is green), someone from the show will come and describe how the show works, the host's approach, the day's topics, who watches, whether there's a live audience and how the host will introduce you. Sometimes, too, hosts will drop by to say hello and thank you for coming.

The review process is an exchange of important information. This is the point where guests can correct introductions, suggest or refine questions for the host and better understand the host's interests and goals.

Makeup.   Adjacent to the green room, typically, is a makeup room, complete with a table, mirror, lights and a makeup person who is there to render you camera-ready. The catch is that not all guests like the makeup process.

- Some guests don't normally wear makeup and feel self-conscious.
- Some guests wear makeup but prefer their talents to those of the makeup artist.
- Some guests are allergic to makeup (although most studio makeup is designed to avoid allergies).
- Some guests wonder how this stuff comes off before either going back on the street or meeting one's spouse.

The purpose of makeup is to highlight good features while hiding beard lines, bags under the eyes, teenage skin eruptions, dueling scars, etc. In addition to the usual profusion of creams, powders, talcs, liners and astringents found in most studios, makeup artists often prepare their own custom-made and homegrown solutions and chemicals, including, at one station, an ominous grey aerosol can marked only as "human dulling spray."

Although the precise contents of this can were never disclosed to me, its purpose was clear. It seems that some male guests have expansive and shiny bald pates, and since something must be done to prevent studio lights from reflecting back into the cameras, human dulling spray was born.

IN THE TV STUDIO

If there is a single quality that makes television unlike other media encounters, it's the matter of distractions. If you haven't been on television, think of it as a job interview conducted in the middle of a rocket launch. As you speak and attempt to present a positive image, all around floor directors are pointing, technicians are adjusting, cameras are aiming while you sit deep in prayer hoping that each of your answers suggests some glimmer of intelligence.

The good news about television is that once you're on the air, everyone wants you to succeed. If you do well, the show does well. But television is a high-tech marvel and it takes a lot of people, equipment and dollars to make the marvel work. To be successful you've got to follow the lead set by your host and floor directors.

Once you move from the green room to the set you'll be fitted with a microphone, told where to sit or stand and where to face. More complex, however, is what happens after the initial setup.

All your life you've been told to be polite and face people when you speak to them, but suddenly you may be in an environment where you're asked to speak to your host while looking elsewhere. "Elsewhere" is a camera that doesn't give cues or responses. You're talking, but the camera doesn't blink, shake its head or laugh.

A studio audience largely eliminates the response problem. You can see or sense a reaction to your words. But in a studio without a live audience, the lack of response can be unsettling because the customary clues by which we measure personal communication are missing.

Worse still are situations where you're separated from both the host and the studio. You may be seated in a room off the set, placed in front of a camera and asked to answer questions that come in over an earphone. Viewers see both you and the host at the same time, but you see nothing. Again, clues to measure performance are missing.

Studios today typically have three cameras and where you look is determined by a floor director who points in one direction or another. The floor director's nods, gestures and signals should be clear but they can also be distracting as you try to answer the host's questions.

When in doubt, or when the floor director's signals are unclear and you're speaking live before 20 million people, talk to the host. It's natural and the control room should be able to find a decent shot, unless you're espousing some cause that infuriates the crew, such as an end to television unions.

Because TV is an unfamiliar environment, practice sessions have become increasingly common. Large corporations often prepare key executives for television with full-scale practice interviews, complete with actual studios, cameras, crews, lights and current or former TV reporters who act as hosts.

Organized by specialized commercial services, such sessions duplicate broadcast conditions and provide realistic feedback for would-be media stars.

Less formal—and less costly—is the use of a simple video camera and monitor. With the widespread availability of video equipment, promoters in every income bracket can now practice their television techniques, respond to questions and see how they look and sound on camera. In the best situations, video practice sessions can be organized by TV consultants who show clients how to make stronger and more effective presentations.

C H A P T E R

7

Breaking into Print

While radio and television have become increasingly important, the printed word remains a powerful promotional tool. Print media are important because they not only have the capacity to convey vast amounts of information, they also offer advantages that radio and television cannot duplicate.

To start, print media coverage is physically tangible. If you see an item of interest you can cut it out, save it, file it or send it to someone else. The ability to save broadcast material is less practical. You could tape the nightly news and save the stories that you like, but few people take the time or make such an effort.

Print media often contain an index or table of contents, something largely unknown on radio or television. The national news may be broadcast at 6:30, but there's no way to tell what each night's coverage may include, or the order in which stories will be presented. With print media, it's easy to look up old stories or particular articles, something of value to promoters who want their words and ideas remembered.

Perhaps the most important advantage enjoyed by print media is the simple fact that most people who today are in their 40s, 50s, and 60s—the very people most likely to make purchasing decisions—grew up in an era when print was primary.

For at least the next 20 or 30 years a large and important segment of the population will remain print oriented.

Attracting print coverage requires a different set of strategies than either radio and television. In the usual case there is more time to develop print stories and more outlets to consider. One need not be photogenic to attain print coverage and sound bites are largely irrelevant.

What counts with the print media is the ability to create a story of interest to readers. Show reporters how readers benefit and your name will soon be in the news.

NEWSPAPERS

If you look back over the past 40 years you can see an interesting phenomenon. Despite the growth of TV and the emergence of the cable industry, daily papers are not only with us, they're flourishing as well.

Although there are many newspapers, big paper competition has declined. In the central cities we see fewer and fewer markets that are competitive in a traditional sense. As of late mid-1990, according to Joe Lorfano, a spokesman for the American Newspaper Publishers Association, only 41 cities had competing dailies and, of these, 21 had joint operating agreements under which printing facilities and other non-editorial assets are shared. The end result is that in 1990 only 20 U.S. cities had at least two independently owned and operated papers.

But although we have fewer competitive dailies, the information industry—of which the daily press is a part—is hardly comatose. We may have fewer competing dailies, but there's no lack of entertainment weeklies, suburban dailies, city magazines, business journals, foreign-language publications, religious papers and free advertisers—many established in just the past few years.

Thus despite dwindling numbers, daily papers still face substantial competition. They may be the largest players on the local field, but they're hardly the monopoly of which ideologues complain and their turf and territory are not immune to competition. Hometown Goliaths must produce a viable product each day or lose readers and advertising to more specialized competitors.

To fight the new competitors, daily papers are becoming increasingly segmented. Monday business sections are now common as are weekend inserts on Fridays. When there isn't enough advertising to justify a weekly section, irregular supplements are produced for such topics as new cars, resort living and computers.

Not only are papers becoming increasingly segmented, they're becoming regionalized as well. There are suburban sections and mid-city editions, each with a somewhat different slant.

What does it mean to promoters?

First, the public still wants its daily paper. Selling 60 million of anything is an achievement, selling 60 million papers each day is remarkable.

Second, papers need massive volumes of material to fill the thousands of pages they produce each day. As a comparison, the script for a 30-minute TV newscast can fit comfortably on one or two pages of a daily paper. Because papers need so much material, there are many opportunities for promoters.

Third, non-daily print outlets should not be ignored. Not only can they provide valued coverage, they can also perk the interest of daily writers. A feature that appears in a suburban weekly can often be rewritten for use by a big-city daily.

Fourth, because of segmentation, daily papers are not monolithic enterprises where a story rejected by one writer is doomed forever. A story that doesn't work on the business pages can often be repackaged as a metro feature, style article, etc.

The process of obtaining newspaper coverage begins with a careful review of target publications. Which sections are most desirable? Are there particular writers who cover your field? Have competitors received coverage and, if so, how much and what kind?

It's worth going to a library and reading back over past stories. You may find a pattern of coverage; you'll surely find good background material to help build a news package.

In broad terms, promoters will want to contact reporters (who cover breaking news), feature writers (who write longer, less time-sensitive pieces), editors, deputy editors and assignment editors (who assign stories) and columnists (who produce commentaries). If you have a story that can be packaged for the business, metro, real estate or feature sections, or perhaps even as breaking news for the first section, you may have five or ten potential contacts to consider with a large city newspaper.

Who gets your first promotional letter?

Pick the section that most interests you and which rationally is most likely to provide coverage. Call up, ask who assigns stories and write that person. Or, if there's *one* reporter you feel would be particularly interested, phone him or her to see if an information package is desired.

What happens next is uncertain. A daily paper has the capacity to publish material overnight or even in a later edition. Sometimes though, stories languish for days or weeks and then promoters have practical problems that aren't always easy to resolve. Here are some examples:

- You've spoken to a writer, found there was interest, sent materials but heard nothing after three weeks. Do you call? Write again? Contact someone else? There's no universal answer, but if you haven't had a response after a week or two, it's not unfair to call and ask if the writer got the materials and still has interest in the story.

- A feature writer likes your story, gets your news package, interviews you at length but no story appears for five weeks. Now what? Do you call? Complain? Contact another writer on the same paper? At this point it's fair to call the first reporter. It may be that the story did not work out, an editor didn't like the article or the editorial calendar is filled for the next month. You *can't* contact another writer until you know the first story's fate. If you interest another reporter and the first story is published elsewhere in the paper, reporter number two is going to be more than annoyed. Conversely, if the second reporter writes about you in one section while the feature article is still in storage somewhere, reporter number one is going to be upset.

- In those few cities where daily papers compete (and sometimes where a city daily competes with suburban papers) there is an unwritten, but very clear, "first interview" rule. If one paper doesn't get the first interview, it won't write about you.

What happens if you're interviewed by one paper, the article is delayed and so you do a story with a competing paper that's published first? The folks at the first paper may be upset, which is a serious problem, but at some point there needs to be a clause to the first interview rule, what might be called the "use it quickly and don't sit on it" statute. Under this regulation, reporters invoking the first interview rule must be prepared to deliver prompt coverage or forfeit their right to exclusivity.

In thinking about local newspaper coverage, daily big city papers often receive lavish attention while suburban papers are largely ignored. This is a mistake because suburban papers have much to offer. In their own right they're often large and sophisticated publications, and while they may not be the biggest paper in a given market, they do attract strong reader support.

What suburban papers typically offer is comprehensive localized coverage coupled with area advertising.

The process and procedure for getting suburban coverage parallels the strategy used for major dailies. Find out who assigns stories, who writes them and contact the right people. Be aware, however, that as papers get smaller, coverage gets more localized. If you can specifically relate your story idea to the geographic area served by a suburban paper, your chances of coverage will greatly improve.

Once you obtain newspaper coverage, a delightful question arises: When should you again seek coverage in the same publication?

Articles, particularly breaking stories, do beget follow-up pieces and it's conceivable you could appear in print the next day. More plausibly, there won't be a follow-up piece and you'll have to search for coverage from another angle or with a different emphasis. When to ask for coverage again will depend on the original article's length and content. If it was a huge feature requiring lots of space and editorial time, renewed coverage may be six months or a year in the future. A short piece may limit coverage from one to three months. Your name buried once in the midst of an article should not be regarded as a bar to additional coverage a week later.

MAGAZINES

Pick any subject, find any viewpoint and there's sure to be magazine coverage somewhere. Having so many publications means not only that every conceivable topic is covered, but also that promoters have a vast number of forums in which to seek exposure.

To earn magazine coverage one must first identify publications of interest. If you have something new for CB radios, for instance, you'll want to target CB, electronic and automotive publications. But these publications, of which there are dozens, represent only a starting point. In addition, there are trade and technical journals, wholesaler and retailer publications, industry magazines and a huge number of secondary targets, such as *Popular Science* in this case, that may give coverage but are not primarily concerned with CBs. If the product is sufficiently unique, it might even be possible to realistically view the major newsweeklies—*Newsweek, Time* and *U.S. News & World Report*—as promotional targets as well.

Magazines do not offer the immediacy of radio, TV or daily newspapers and that is their strength. Magazines typically have longer deadlines (publication in two months rather than tomorrow), which means they are able to take a different approach to news gathering. (It should be said that with computerized typesetting plus satellite transmissions, some magazines can be written almost overnight. This is not the usual case, however.)

The attraction of long lead times is that many magazines (but not all) can be approached months before you're ready to "go public." You can get feedback from reporters, test promotional ideas, and if your marketing approach doesn't get results with magazines, perhaps adjustments can be made before going to newspapers or the electronic media.

As a promoter you may want your magazine story in print by a particular time, say early December. That may require promotional efforts one, two or three months in advance, but since there are no guarantees, what happens if December rolls around and none of the 42 magazines you contacted print anything?

Or what if they print your story in the January edition? Unless you're hot, you may be bumped for a more important story or, if ad sales are poor, because the "book's" size is limited.

Although promoters often want coverage by a certain date, one can argue that the long deadlines and variable schedules offered by magazines are ultimately beneficial.

Imagine a situation where every publication and media outlet publishes or airs your story in a single week. This may seem like a terrific accomplishment, but ask yourself a question: What were the three top news stories two weeks ago? Five weeks ago? Do you remember? What happens if the week your story was publicized the country was absorbed with a plane disaster or international crisis? Sure, you've got clippings and videos, but have you maximized promotional opportunities?

Unless you have a one-time event (Circus comes to town Friday. Be there!), promotional efforts are most effective over a period of weeks, months and possibly years—an evolutionary process in which magazines fit perfectly. Coverage may be stretched over time, but *a mix of stories in various media is itself an index of credibility*. The promoter who scores big in a single week may have a fad, while the publicist who gets coverage week after week will certainly enjoy greater credibility and more opportunities for success than the seven-day wonder.

Look at almost any magazine and you can quickly see how coverage is typically divided into current events, feature stories, interviews, pictorials, columns of analysis and opinion plus brief updates on a variety of topics, each covered in a single paragraph. Such formula production suggests that promoters should not only direct their attention to certain magazines, but also to specific sections and forms of coverage within each publication.

Few general magazines offer current events coverage in the sense of breaking news because production deadlines allow radio, TV and newspapers to reach the public more quickly. Specialized journals, however, are themselves often sources of hard news because they thoroughly cover given areas. The *New England Journal of Medicine* is constantly in the news because it carries front-running health coverage.

Feature stories, in-depth articles that may run for thousands of words, are a magazine staple. These are the long articles in the middle of the "book" and usually featured on the front cover, the stories that most reflect a publication's ideas, attitudes and interests. Feature stories are hard to develop and therefore magazines are always looking for new ideas, particularly publications that cover specialized fields.

New feature material can often be made from updated past stories. Most magazines seem to work on a two- or three-year cycle, so a story that ran several years ago may be updated and used again, with new sources and the latest information.

Magazines often feature regular interview sections and coverage here can establish promoters as authority figures. (If you're quoted in a national magazine you must know something, right?) It's not easy for most of us to suggest ourselves as interview subjects, but such gracious offers are unnecessary. Instead what usually happens is that an interview arises as an alternative to feature coverage because it's sometimes easier to cover a topic with a question and answer format. In addition, if a subject is sufficiently famous, an interview format creates exclusivity and bragging rights for the publication ("Elvis Back from the Dead, Read His Fascinating Interview Exclusively in the Crystal Ball Weekly").

Interview pieces are typically tape-recorded, transcribed and edited, at which point the subject is sent a transcript to review. Reviewing makes great sense since substance and continuity can be lost when a wide-ranging, two-hour interview is boiled down to 1,500 words.

Magazines have a unique capacity to publish photos and some publications dazzle the eye with their graphic work. If you want your picture used, make sure it's either an 8" × 10" black-and-white glossy or else a 35mm color slide. Whether you provide pictures or the publication sends over a photographer, the same standards apply: Find interesting locations and backgrounds, look for unique angles and avoid mundane "head shots" best saved for obituary columns. If you supply the photo, be certain to have a credit line such as "Source: T.W. Baker Company."

Magazines often receive information they want to cover, but not with a full-scale story. One approach to such stories is to reduce them to a paragraph or less for a capsule column. Such features are well read because they're short, easy to absorb and to the point. Getting capsule coverage often takes no more than an interesting news release, but a well-written letter to the writer is probably a better bet. If the writer is unknown and the column is called "Capsule Comments" or whatever, just write to "Capsule Editor." It'll get to the right hands.

Magazine columnists, like commentators everywhere, can write about everything and everyone. Other than the limits of libel, there are no guidelines for columnists and it's a mistake to believe that columnists must be fair or impartial. Their job is to present an opinion, a bias, often saying things that cannot or should not be said in news columns or feature articles.

Coverage by columnists is best obtained by the simple expedient of sitting down and writing a letter. Rather than writing about yourself ("Gee, please write about me in your column because I've been in this business for six years...") it's best to comment on a subject: "I was interested in your September column, which discussed educational efforts in our industry. We don't know if it's the best solution for everyone, but we have a somewhat different training approach: When a new agent joins our firm, we pair that individual with one of our veterans. They share office space, have the same hours and work jointly on projects. We find that both benefit because..." A columnist not interested in pursuing the topic is likely use the letter elsewhere or send it over to another writer.

NEWSLETTERS

With so much attention given to newspapers, magazines and the electronic media it's easy to overlook subscription newsletters. Newsletters, after all, aren't at your local newsstand, rarely carry advertising and often have circulations of less than several thousand readers. In the context of media outlets reaching millions of people, newsletters *seem* unimportant—at least to the unwary.

And yet it's a mistake to view newsletters lightly. Newsletters are significant, not because they reach a huge audience (although some have six-figure subscription levels), but because they're often the fastest and most effective way to reach selected readership groups.

Newsletters rarely carry ads. Editorial copy, usually four to eight tightly written pages, doesn't compete with advertising for reader attention or time and the physical size and concentrated content of subscription newsletters creates a unique news product. Items appearing in newsletters are read if only because there are few distractions. Similar material in a big-city newspaper or major magazine may be buried and unnoticed amid 100 pages of editorial clutter.

What makes subscription newsletters important is that such publications must have clear editorial merit to survive. A newsletter that publishes material from last week's paper can be described in one word: Defunct.

Not only must newsletters be fresh and original, they must offer one or more additional values as well.

Specialization.   By providing information not typically or fully carried by papers and magazines, newsletters are a preferred channel of information, sometimes the only channel, for certain industries, professions and groups. A lawsuit involving an environmental issue, for example, may not make the papers generally, even though it is important to certain business interests and environmental organizations. Newsletters serving such fields will fully report the suit and its implications.

Advanced information.   Newsletters often lure readers with coverage found elsewhere, but found later. The benefit to readers is that by having advanced information, they're able to anticipate trends. If you know the Jones Company has made progress with an anti-cancer drug, that's important for competitors, stock analysts, physicians, pharmacists and patients.

Expertise.   Subscription newsletters are typically written by reporters with extensive training and experience who cover a single subject. Between their background, concentration and contacts, such writers are authorities within given fields. Moreover, because they're journalists, they have access to information and people who would not normally be available to competitors in a particular area.

Need.   You won't find too much in the local paper, but if you want to vacation on a freighter, there's a monthly newsletter on the subject. Often a topic is so specialized that the potential universe of readers could not justify newspaper or magazine support, so newsletters—with their low production costs and ability to specialize—are perfect vehicles to reach small groups such as those who want to follow injection molding trends, learn more about intellectual property decisions or keep up with the potato industry.

Exclusivity.   A key feature offered or implied by many newsletters is an "inside" perspective, information that will immediately and instantaneously put you at the center of a given field or activity. What's going on, how to save, who to contact, what to expect—all rendered with detail and clarity—are the mainstays of many letters.

Contacting a newsletter editor requires nothing more than finding appropriate letters in various directories and then sending a brief letter and background materials to the editor or publisher.

But if contacting newsletters is easy, getting coverage is tough. Newsletters have little space and what they use must not only interest their readers, it must also appear in print before it reaches the general media. Relative to the space available, there's tremendous competition for coverage. Thus, promoters are most likely to succeed if they package their material for each newsletter they contact and then send it out so it can be published before reaching the general media.

Desktop Publishing

With computers becoming as common as house plants, the opportunity to self-publish newsletters has increased enormously. Combine layout and design programs with laser printers and results impossible just a few years ago can be achieved easily.

While technology has advanced, artistry has not and therein lies a problem. Too many do-it-yourself newsletters feature primitive designs and unattractive typesetting.

What to do? Go to a design class at a local college or university and find out why it is that some layouts work better than others. The answers are surprising, such matters as how the eye moves, the way we read, and how the mind absorbs information.

In addition to seeking newsletter coverage, promoters might also consider another tack: Self-publishing. If the particular audience you want is sufficiently important, if your story is ongoing and if you need to be in front of a specific audience on a frequent basis—it may make sense to start your own newsletter.

In the megabuck world of modern media the opportunity to own or start a publication or broadcast outlet is largely reserved for the well-heeled. But although existing print and electronic properties in major markets are often worth hundreds of millions of dollars, newsletters remain the one area within journalism where anyone with ideas and a mailing list has the potential to be immediately competitive.

A captive newsletter can be enormously enticing for several reasons.

First, you control the editorial content. Whatever you want in print is written to your requirements.

Second, you have a regular forum to reach specific readers.

Third, you can extend your forum to others by offering space for guest editorials, free classifieds, salary surveys, a job mart or whatever. Such features provide an element of editorial validity not otherwise feasible in a publication devoted solely to you and your interests.

Fourth, as a publisher you may be regarded as an authority figure in your field by general-outlet reporters, someone to be interviewed and consulted.

Over time, your letter may evolve into an editorial product of such value that you can actually charge subscription fees. Lest this sound uninteresting, consider that successful newsletters probably represent the highest rate of return on invested capital that one can postulate in the media business. Few dollars and little equipment are needed up-front, just labor and that most precious of all media commodities: Well-packaged ideas.

CHAINS, SYNDICATES AND NETWORKS

A large portion of all editorial coverage comes not from local reporters at a given publication or station, but from outside sources such as wire services, syndicates, chains and networks. Large newspaper groups often have their own wire services. Central news bureaus and papers within groups routinely swap stories. Numerous media services serve hundreds of independent papers. In a parallel manner, radio and television stations are often owned by a single corporate entity and yet they too can plug into a variety of networks, syndications and services.

News services and networks have a profound effect on the news gathering process. It's very expensive to send a reporter or camera crew to cover a given story, particularly if that same story is already being covered by a service to which the paper or station subscribes. Besides, it's the development of stories not found on the news services or networks that give local media outlets dimension and distinction.

Although news services have central staffs to generate material, they also have other sources. Many take local stories and revise them for wider publication or broadcast. Alternatively, local reporters take their own stories and revise them for a service. With feature stories the process is often easier since revision may not be required. A story on auto safety or beating holiday doldrums could run anywhere.

Local reporters may be easier to reach than central news services, but wire-service journalists also face a competitive problem. News service time and space are tight, especially since national wire services run news for the entire country.

But even if a story runs on a news service, that does not mean it will run in 50 cities, or even in one. The story must still be selected from among many choices by local editors. What happens to wire-service copy?

- Some editors will pick out the material and run it.
- Some editors will ignore it.
- Some editors will keep a story for research or background information.
- Some editors will assign reporters to devise localized articles on the same subjects.

The bottom line: News service coverage guarantees widespread distribution, not necessarily publication space or broadcast time.

Suppose Ms. Williams develops computer software that allows children to quickly and easily understand basic math. To promote her creation Williams devises a simple plan: She'll mail out review copies with a cover letter to the media and hope for coverage.

Williams could send copies to the nation's 1,200 TV stations, 10,000 radio stations, 1,700 daily papers, 7,500 weekly papers, 5,000 commercial newsletters, 5,000-plus magazines and 20,000 association publications. However, Williams—not having been mentioned in the wills of the rich or famous—must limit her marketing effort to 100 media outlets. Which outlets does she choose?

One category, certainly, would include the five or ten leading educational publications, particularly those going to elementary school math instructors. A second category would encompass newsletters and magazines that serve the computer education and retailing market. Media that serve bookstores generally and children's bookstores in particular would be a third choice.

To this point, Williams has mailed 80 of her 100 precious disks. Her approach has been to directly influence educational authorities and retailers, but she also needs to reach end users or, in this case, their parents, so she can stimulate public demand.

Williams finds 20 news services, chains and bureaus in various directories and asks for the names of those covering educational or scientific issues. She finds that most services have such specialists and sends each a copy of her program along with a letter, news release and short background paper entitled, "From Fingers to Figures: Math Made Simple."

The competition for news service time and attention is extremely tough but Williams has followed a reasonable procedure to gain coverage. She located the services most likely to reach worthwhile outlets. She asked for the right people to contact, prepared separate news packages for each and wrote individual letters.

It's entirely possible that only one of her 20 service contacts will elect to write a story. It's also possible that the one story produced will appear in 150 outlets. Thus the fact that chains, news services and networks exist is a big plus not only for local media, but for promoters as well. They create still another media target, one that allows promoters to reach many markets at once and with greatly reduced promotional costs as a result.

C H A P T E R

8

Advertorials

A new form of literature has emerged in the past few years, something called an "advertorial." Instead of having independent editorial material surrounded by ads, advertorials are publications or programs where the editorial content is controlled, influenced or actually produced by advertisers.

Whether advertorials should be classified as advertising or as media marketing is a matter of debate. More certain, however, is the idea that properly constructed advertorials offer interesting promotional opportunities.

Advertisers like advertorials because the copy is "safe" (read: uncritical and non-controversial). No need to worry about investigative reporters; none would work for advertorials. Advertorials are also attractive because they offer a "shopping mall" effect; many competitors in a single place produce more business than competing shops spread over a wide area.

Advertorials raise a basic question for promoters: If advertorials are such a good idea then how can you make use of them? The answer will vary according to the dollars available and the media selected.

Print. Used as inserts in newspapers and magazines, advertorials commonly focus on such single-subject topics as health,

An Insider's View of Advertorials

As a free-lance editor I have produced some of the largest newspaper advertorial packages published in the United States. These glossy, four-color, magazine-style sections on fine paper are complex products that frequently contain editorial contributions from sophisticated promoters. As an editor, here's what I look for when dealing with a contributor.

Expertise. The writer—or at least the person who receives credit for the article or column—must have appropriate credentials. Lawyers, doctors and businesspeople can all qualify.

Submission. All materials must be received on time, on hard copy, and on an IBM-compatible disk in the form of an ASCII file.

Editing. All materials will be edited for style (to conform with the general standards for newspapers and magazines) and clarity.

Galleys. Authors will receive edited galleys by fax. They must be reviewed and returned within 24 hours or it will be assumed that no changes are required. At this point it is understood that additional editing may be needed, that copy may

cars and high-tech employment. The sections, which are usually marked as "an advertising supplement to the *Vine Street Gazette*" or—in small type on each page—as "advertising," feature editorial material surrounded by ads. The editorial material may range in content from overt promotional fare (one article per advertiser, or an "editorial" mention for each display ad) to more sophisticated copy that would conceivably fit in regular editorial sections.

Unless an organization or person is funding an advertorial individually, print advertorials are likely to be sections that group advertisers with a common theme. To gain coverage in this media, speak to an advertising representative or supplement manager and have the advertorial calendar for the year sent to you.

If there are upcoming advertorials of interest you might then offer to write *editorial* copy for the section, a strategy that

---

An Insider's View of Advertorials (continued)

still be cut, and that the material may or may not be used. Advertorial contributions are, at bottom, a gamble.

Rights. Rights to advertorial contributions generally are ceded to the newspaper that produces the section, though this is negotiable. As an alternative, it can be arranged for the local paper to have a one-time right to use the material.

Reproduction. A promoter will typically need the paper's permission to reprint his or her contribution. This should be worked out in writing prior to publication.

Payment. Promoters are not paid for their time, effort or contributions. The view is that if a promoter's work is used, the promoter will benefit.

Photos. When submitting photos, promoters should be certain that they, in fact, own the pictures they wish to contribute. If a professional photographer has taken the pictures, then there should be a clear written statement showing that either the promoter owns the photos or has the photographer's permission to use them in the advertorial. Credit lines are required for all photos.

---

can produce three benefits. First, you can be seen as an authority figure in your field. Second, given a proper identification, you can get business ("This article was written by Lemuel Jones, owner of LJ's Wine and Cheese Shop on Main Street."). Third, in the usual case you don't have to pay for the space occupied by your advertorial copy.

If not a story, see what else is needed. Perhaps you can supply an interview, photo, diagram or table. At least take the time to ask about advertorials—few people do and the result is that few people gain coverage.

Television.   TV advertorials are typically half-hour or hour-length commercials where favored subjects seem to be hair restoration, kitchen appliances and instant millions from real estate investing. Some TV advertorials, such as certain wrestling shows, are so popular they even garner sponsors! If there's a heaven for ad agencies it must surely consist of advertisers sponsoring advertisements that are popular with the public.

Another TV approach is the advertorial interview. Here the "guest" is interviewed by a "host" who tells you in great detail how the guest's product, service or book can be ordered. The orders go to an address or phone controlled by the host, who then lops off a percentage of the take before passing the balance to the guest.

There are few advertorials on local television at this writing other than real estate shows. Real estate programs feature either the listings of one company or one franchise network so obviously there is no room for a competitor. If a local real estate association organizes an advertorial then members may have access to TV time, something likely to become more common in the future.

The bottom line with television: Unless you have big bucks, there are few opportunities with TV advertorials.

Radio.   Radio advertorials consist of blocks of time usually controlled by a single advertiser. An insurance company might buy an hour of airtime each Monday at 3 P.M. or whenever. The company can hire a host, control the show's content, name guests and even run ads on its own program. Other than an oblique announcement ("The views expressed on this program do not necessarily reflect the opinion of this station or its sponsors..."), radio listeners are often unaware that the program is controlled by the advertiser rather than the station.

Many promoters can afford to purchase a regular block of radio time and such advertorial programming is often a good media buy. A better deal is to get on someone else's advertorial program. While a direct competitor won't have you as a guest, many shows want "experts" and authority figures to interview and to answer caller questions. In some cases it is possible to get booked on an advertorial radio show if you can enhance the show. For example, a CPA, lawyer or financial planner might appear on a real estate, insurance or banking program. Such experts can add to the program's content while not taking business from the promoter.

Should Advertorials Replace the News?

As media outlets search for more profits there is sometimes an urge to replace editorial matter with advertorial sections, the latter being more profitable and far less difficult to produce. Some newspaper real estate sections, for example, are produced by advertising departments and other papers may be considering such transitions.

The trouble is that advertorials, no matter how well developed, are simply a form of advertising. They do not offer the objectivity, independence or adversarial stance that editorial materials naturally represent.

There is a place for advertorials, but only in those cases where the commercial nature of the product is plainly identified. Conversely, there is no excuse for replacing editorial material with advertising copy.

Advertisers and promoters who don't like those pesky and sometimes "negative" reporters should consider what would happen if editorial efforts were replaced with advertorial materials. The national "news" would be written by political parties, the TV section would be generated by networks, the food section by agribusinesses, and the sports pages would be filled with handouts from local teams. There would be something for everyone willing to pay, but nothing for anyone who simply wanted an independent view of the world.

Newsletters. Another approach to advertorials is the captive newsletter. While such letters offer "safe" editorial matter, the package of values they provide differs somewhat from other advertorial formats. Captive letters typically have only one sponsor and thus offer exclusivity. Because they're newsletters, they can be quickly and inexpensively produced. Last, captive newsletters can be issued on a regular schedule to reinforce messages or on an as-needed basis for seasonal events.

Advertorials offer exposure and the possibility for exposure should not be ignored. Many people have been successful with advertorials and the same strategies that work with media marketing in general can sometimes be applied to advertorials as well.

C H A P T E R

9

Evaluation

At some point in every media marketing program, time must be set aside to consider results: What was accomplished, how could you have done better and what are your next steps?

Evaluation should be used to measure past performance and devise future strategies. Knowing what worked—and what didn't—can be crucially important as new programs are developed.

Yet measuring media marketing results is often difficult because the purpose of a given campaign may be expressed in terms that are hard to quantify. How do you measure "an enhanced corporate image" or "better employee morale"?

Even if you can see results through burgeoning sales or surveys that show improved public perceptions, are you measuring the correct issues? How much of your new-found success was a result of your media marketing campaign and how much was caused by factors outside your control, general trends that carried you along?

As an example, one measure of employee morale might be reduced worker separations. If people stay with your firm in higher numbers than before, do you not have evidence that employee morale is on the upswing? Maybe. But what if unemployment rates are generally rising and as a result those with jobs are now holding on, fearing they might not find employment elsewhere?

More complex still are campaigns that involve the use of both media marketing and paid advertising. You know someone saw your ad if 5,000 coupons are returned. But did they respond because the advertisement itself was innately interesting, or because your media marketing effort created a receptive environment? Given the dollars spent, do 5,000 coupons constitute a good response in any case?

Measuring results is more complicated than looking at raw numbers. Have the right questions been asked? Were the correct people polled? Have the results been interpreted correctly? Analysis and context are no less important than basic data.

If it's at all possible, the best environment in which to measure media marketing results is one without advertising. One medical products firm, for example, had no advertising funds or sales staff. But within its limit budget, the company developed a media marketing campaign that generated coverage in local, national and professional publications. Within a year, sales tripled and the firm moved to larger quarters. Assuming constant demand, there was no factor other than media marketing to account for this sudden growth spurt.

Every six months or so, before going any further with your marketing campaign, it pays to sit down, write out your goals, and then note your accomplishments. Accomplishments include not only articles and interviews but also such fundamental activities as identifying media outlets and developing a complete media package. Here is a general checklist for professionals and business owners.

1. Have you developed an angle? Why is it that reporters should be interested in you or your product or service? How will readers, listeners and viewers benefit from the information you offer journalists? Have journalists shown an interest in the angle you've selected? If not, maybe another approach is needed.

2. Have you developed a news release? What words have you put on paper to describe your story? Is your release interesting? Provocative? Newsworthy? Purely self-serving? How

have journalists responded to your release? If the response has been weak, maybe the release should be rewritten.

3. Have you developed a media contact list? Raw numbers are not important, only quality counts. Do your media outlets reach the potential customers and clients you want to influence? Have the reporters you contacted shown an interest in your materials? If not, maybe you have the wrong list.

4. Have you developed supporting materials such as histories, background papers, brief bios? What about photos, slides or illustrations? Have reporters said they read such materials and have they been used in stories? If not, new background materials may be required.

5. Within given media outlets, have you identified assignment editors and individual reporters to contact? How often do you update your list? Don't write to reporters who no longer work for given media outlets and make sure the addresses you have are current and correct. If a reporter has changed jobs, would the new position continue to make him or her a valued media contact? If so, expand your mailing list. (Coworkers at old publications and stations will routinely give out new phone numbers and addresses for past workers as a matter of courtesy.)

6. After you have received coverage, have you called or written the journalist to say what response you received?

7. Have you seen competitors obtain media coverage in outlets not on your list or with different news values? Should you adjust your strategy?

8. How has your media relations campaign influenced clients, customers, employees and competitors? How do you feel about your efforts?

9. How should you refine your promotional efforts during the next six months to obtain better results?

10. Relax. Media marketing programs are never finalized. They continue as long as you're in business and they must be changed and updated constantly.

After reviewing your program and its results, don't be surprised if changes are required. Media marketing is not a stagnant science; experience plus ever-changing conditions mean that media marketing programs *should* evolve. Promotional programs need to be fresh, innovative and clever; they must change and grow; and the need for change is what makes good promotion a challenge and a satisfaction.

A P P E N D I X

Developing Model Programs

Media marketing programs range in size from two-page letters to massive documents not much smaller than community phone books. Regardless of size, all programs must first analyze problems and then offer detailed solutions based on media marketing principles.

How does an actual program look? What does it say? The best way to find out is to examine realistic models. In the section that follows we've outlined programs for a real estate broker, an insurance agency, a banker and an association.

The plans are organized with program elements first and then likely actions and responses later. Although the organizations, individuals and specific situations described in the following programs are entirely fictitious, some elements and wording have been used in actual proposals.

PARROTT REALTY

Real estate brokerage is a nationwide service business with competitors ranging in size from independent operators to corporate giants. Licensed in every state, brokers represent other parties for a fee in the purchase, sale, management, rental and exchange of real estate.

Parrott Realty is a mid-sized firm with one broker and ten agents, located in a suburban community. The company seeks to list and sell single-family homes, residential condominiums and small commercial buildings.

In business for nearly 20 years, the company now faces new competition. A discount broker has begun to fight with Parrott for listings and the company's best agent has been approached by several firms willing to offer higher commission splits. To make matters more difficult, a recession has reduced overall market activity, homes are on the market longer, and listings are more expensive to carry than in the past.

Find the Media

The company president, Steve Parrott, surveyed all relevant media in his service area and found that his market is served by one major daily paper, one large suburban daily, six weekly papers, 18 radio stations, one city magazine, one business weekly, six television stations, four local cable systems and one college weekly. The daily papers and weeklies have business sections. Two papers publish large real estate sections. Three TV stations have news operations and four produce local interview programs. The city magazine has a personal finance and real estate feature each month. The business weekly has a commercial real estate section. Two radio stations offer "all-talk" programming. Each cable outlet has local interview programming, plus two cable systems make facilities available for local individuals and groups to produce their own programming. The contact list has 120 names when completed.

Establish a Direction

Parrott realizes that his problems cannot be solved with a few random news clippings, so instead he decides to develop a three-pronged program. First, he will step up direct efforts to gain additional clients. Second, he will seek media attention to establish his credentials as a real estate authority. Third, he will create a new incentive program for his top agent.

Establish a Program

To attract media attention, Parrott needs to stand out from other brokers so he asks an old friend, Mr. Withers, to help. Withers is about to place his home on the market and Parrott wants Withers' permission to have a reporter follow the transaction from listing to closing. Withers agrees with the stipulation that his name cannot be mentioned in any story.

Armed with written permission from Withers, Parrott sends the following letter to Tim Conrad, real estate editor for the nearby big city daily.

Dear Mr. Conrad:

With sales slowing and prices moderating, it's become increasingly difficult to market local homes. That said, homes do sell and your readers might want to follow a model sale to see how the process works. I've obtained written permission from an owner who will soon be selling his home to allow you or one of your reporters to cover the seller's side of the transaction from the inside and to go from the initial listing to marketing, negotiation, financing and on to the final closing.

I expect to list the property within the coming ten days, so if this story idea is of interest, please contact me to work out the details.

Sincerely,
Steve Parrott

Parrott knew that his seller was not in a hurry to list the home so if Conrad did not respond, the letter could be revised and sent to another editor. As it happened the editor liked the idea and a three-part series entitled "Brokers at Work" soon appeared in the real estate section.

While Parrott was sending out his media letter he began to work on a different communication problem. The mails were saturated with materials from brokers who compete with Parrott. There were monthly newsletters, postcards when homes were first listed, more postcards when they sold, and even advertising on the back of grocery store sales slips.

Parrott saved all the mailings from his competitors and spread them out on a large table. Looking at the work before him, Parrott could see that they fell into two groups: professionally prepared materials that involve much time and expense to prepare and cheap fliers that Parrott would not use because they did not reflect the professionalism he wants to project.

What struck Parrott most about the materials he saw was that whether good or bad they were mass-produced. No one actually sat down and thought about client needs. Instead, each pitch was designed to generate business rather than to solve a client's problem. Parrott decided on a different approach.

Rather than a mass mailing he assigned each agent to physically drive down selected streets and list the numbers of attractive homes. A better approach, said several agents, would be to forget the driving and just buy computerized lists of property owners.

Parrott listened to his agents and then presented the advantages of his approach:

- Computerized ownership lists would not show which homes were currently listed by other brokers.
- Computerized lists would not show those houses that had been poorly maintained and thus least likely to sell in a short amount of time.
- Computerized lists were used by everyone else.

Once each agent gathered numbers for several streets it was a simple matter to create a mailing list. Parrott developed a computerized data base that showed the street and house numbers, put his list on a portable computer, and then went down to the local courthouse where property owners were listed alphabetically, by tax number, and by street address. Using the street address system he quickly filled in property owner names to match the addresses found by his agents.

Once he had a mailing list, Parrott then produced individually typed letters on a word processor for each owner.

Dear Mr. Smith:

Wouldn't you like to hear something different from a real estate broker?

There's no shortage of brokers, something that must seem obvious from the large number of newsletters, postcards, and fliers you receive each week. But how many brokers take the time to write you individually?

At Parrott Realty we have an old-fashioned view of the real estate business. We believe each client is unique and that every home requires an individually designed marketing program.

Having worked in our community for 20 years we have a backlog of neighborhood friends but we hope that if you need the services of a real estate professional you won't choose us merely because we have an outstanding track record for others. Instead, think about your needs, see how we can best serve your interests, and allow us to establish an outstanding track record with *you.*

If your home is now listed with another broker please disregard this letter; otherwise, please call when you need information or advice concerning the local real estate market.

Sincerely,
Ray Blank

Each letter was individually signed by an agent and then to continue the theme of individual attention, each envelope was mailed with a regular postage stamp, not a postage meter imprint. It was Parrott's hope that his missive would generate one to two listings per hundred letters. In essence, it cost less than $100 for postage and stationery to capture a listing that could yield fees worth several thousand dollars.

To go with his mailing, Parrott took three steps to make his current activities more visible.

First, he traded in his old brown-and-white signs for new ones that featured a "Parrott" in four bright hues. Not only were the signs far more alluring during the day, but because the signs were luminescent, they could be seen at night.

Second, each lawn sign included a small box with fliers describing the property. This idea did not thrill all of Parrott's agents because some argued that a buyer could take a flier and then use another broker to buy the property, thereby reducing the commission that a Parrott agent would receive. Parrott saw the matter differently. To Parrott the important point was to make deals and sell houses. Cooperation with other brokers would ultimately mean more money in everyone's pocket.

Third, Parrott changed the way open houses were conducted. Instead of having only information about the property that was open, Parrott started to cross-sell listings. In other words, at each open house there were uniform sets of information about every Parrott listing.

At this point Parrott had started to work on two of his three concerns—he had contacted the media and he was making new efforts to reach the public. There was still the matter of doing something to retain his top agent, Ms. Travers, and here Parrott decided to use media marketing as well.

While office economics prevented Parrott from making any additional changes in the fee arrangement he had with Travers, he could give her additional market exposure. As a result of the stories run in the real estate section, Parrott found that he was contacted by several radio shows that wanted someone to speak about the local real estate scene. Rather then accepting such opportunities directly, Parrott instead sent Travers.

Before letting Travers represent the firm, however, he gave her careful instructions:

- She was not to mention the firm's name on the air. That way the host would have to explain who Travers was and with whom she worked.
- Travers was not to discuss individual clients by name. It would be fair instead to refer to "colonials priced at $200,000" rather than to discuss a specific listing.

- After each program Travers was to write a brief thank-you note to the host or hostess.

To help Travers further, Parrott also gave her a new title: senior residential specialist. Now Travers could be introduced as a "senior marketing representative with Parrott Realty" rather than as a mere "agent."

Travers, of course, began to gain new business because she was increasingly perceived as a real estate authority. Solid interviews led to more radio programs and within a year she was on the air or in the paper several times a month. While her fee split with Parrott didn't change, her business volume grew and that was a benefit not to be ignored.

Evaluation

Over time Parrott became increasingly well known as a source for reporters and as a broker with a select clientele. But as he reviewed the steps he had taken, he felt he should establish additional programs:

- To keep his name in the news Parrott sent a quarterly summary of story ideas to local reporters. His topics included such subjects as "How To Cut Mortgage Costs by 50 Percent," "Where Local Growth Is Headed," "Ten Ways To Make a Home More Salable," and "What Really Happens at Closing."
- Parrott installed a TDD (Telecommunications Device for the Deaf) in his office so that hearing-impaired individuals could obtain real estate information. To promote this service, Parrott contacted several advocacy groups and social agencies that work with the hearing-impaired. Parrott expected that his TDD would generate additional business, and it did, in large measure because other local brokers failed to serve a community with a need for both housing and specialized communication services.
- Parrott continued his individually addressed and typed letters by assigning agents to canvass new streets each month. In addition, Parrott wrote follow-up letters every six

months—enough to keep in touch but not enough to be a nuisance.

FIFTH NATIONAL

Fifth National is a conservative, mid-sized bank that serves a variety of small cities and towns throughout Lincoln County. The bank is well known, has assets of $150 million, but now faces new competition.

A center-city bank, Worldwide National, with assets of $85 billion has opened six branches in the communities served by Fifth National. The big bank has attracted several major business clients and Fifth National is concerned that its asset base could erode as the big firm opens more branches. Since Fifth National cannot offer lower rates or bigger loans than its huge competitor, it instead elects to use a media marketing campaign to hold its marketplace position. Fifth National's president, Weldon Walker, places himself in charge of the program.

Find the Media

Walker finds that his area is served by one TV station that has broadcast facilities within the country, 21 radio outlets, one major daily paper, a cable system, 22 suburban papers, one city magazine and one weekly business paper. From his research Walker identifies 21 media contacts who specialize in business and finance as well as 46 reporters who cover general community news.

Create a Program

Each month Fifth National sends out 12,000 statements to area savers and borrowers. Walker decides that while the monthly statements have usually included promotional materials, they now need a new orientation. Walker devises a series of coupon-sized promotions that stress local issues and involvements.

"Why go 900 miles for a loan?" asked the first coupon. "At Fifth National we've been serving Lincoln County for 75 years. We grew up in the area, our kids go to the local schools, and we're part of the local community. So when it comes time to buy a home, car or boat, why go long distance? Fifth National offices are open throughout Lincoln County. Right where we've always been."

"Did you ever wonder why old MacDonald has a farm?" asked the second coupon. "A few years ago when farm prices fell, fertilizer prices rose, and equipment costs moved higher, Fred MacDonald could have lost his 150-acre farm over at Knight's Corners. But at Fifth National we know that farmers like Fred have been in the county since it was founded. We also know that farms contribute much to the values that make Lincoln County a good place to live. It was difficult to do, but we were able to help Fred MacDonald keep his farm. It wasn't the kind of deal that would made sense among big-city banks and their in-house number crunchers, but then not too many big-city bankers drive past corn fields on their way to work."

"Sorry," said the third monthly coupon. "Unlike some financial institutions we don't have a fleet of corporate jets, but then Lincoln County where we work is only 82 miles across at its widest point. We also want to apologize to business leaders in Brazil, Poland and Bulgaria, but we only make loans within Lincoln County and nearby communities. And we also want to ask the nation's leading stock market tycoons to forgive us. We don't underwrite corporate buyouts that create millions of dollars on Wall Street and unemployment on Main Street. Main Street, after all, is where our friends and neighbors have been for 75 years."

Walker's next step was to create community-based programs that his large competitor could not duplicate. Fifth National might be small, regional and old, but those were qualities that could be converted into virtues if properly handled.

Walker knew that in a typical year the bank had a 20-percent turnover in personnel. Seen another way, each year 30 people left the bank and since Fifth National had been in business for 75 years, there were a lot of past bank employees who now worked elsewhere in the community.

Given this background Walker announced an "Alumni Checking Program" for anyone who had once worked for the bank. Each individual who signed up would get a free personal checking account as well as free checks.

"Free" checking did not necessarily mean checking accounts that produced no benefits for the bank. While fee income was not generated, other advantages were created.

One form of profit came from an account's "float," the money in a checking account that earned no interest for the customer but did generate interest for the bank. A second form of profit came simply from cross-selling, the bank's effort to market other products to customers with free checking. Car loans, mortgages, home equity financing, certificates of deposit, student loans and safe deposit box rentals were just a few of the additional products offered by the bank.

A third benefit for the bank was somewhat subtle. Free checking provided an introduction to new accounts. Some of the people who received free checking accounts could bring new business to the bank from their professions, stores, community organizations and companies.

As for media relations, Fifth National did well. The program attracted stories in virtually all local papers. Beyond the initial stories, Fifth National received another benefit as well: With permission from past employees, the bank put together a portfolio of "notable alumni," including the oldest ("Banking Before Main Street Was Paved"), the most successful ("Former Bank Clerk Now Employs 200"), and the youngest ("College Student Goes from Banking to Biology").

Another innovation that Walker developed was the Wednesday breakfast group. It worked this way: Each Wednesday morning Walker would invite a select group of business leaders and politicians for an informal, off-the-record breakfast to discuss current events. The idea was to be sociable but also to introduce individuals who might be helpful to one another—and the bank. Over time the bank breakfasts became a much sought-after institution.

While Walker could not invite the entire county to breakfast, he could make the bank more accessible. One step was to create the "Monday Open House," which allowed customers to

Fifth National
1 Main Street
Lincoln City, MD 20902

Contact: Amanda Samuels
307-720-2500 (Office)
307-720-1451 (Fax)
301-481-9382 (Home)

FOR IMMEDIATE RELEASE:

Banking before Main Street Was Paved

When Albert Grumby first came to Lincoln County at the age of two, horses could still be hitched on Main Street, the "old" Lincoln Elementary School had just opened, and the second Roosevelt would not be president for several years.

"My family moved to Lincoln because there were jobs and we could grow much of our own food on three acres just outside of town," said Grumby. "We used to skinny-dip at the pond on Connor's Acres, shop at the farmers' market that was set up each Saturday on Main Street, and later, when I was a teenager, I got a job after school working at Fifth National. Instead of computers, each teller had an abacus to balance accounts, a system that worked surprisingly well."

At 86, Grumby is the oldest area resident to qualify for Fifth National's alumni checking program. Having employed more than 1,500 local residents during its 75-year history, Fifth National in May announced that all former employees would be entitled to free checking as long as they lived in the Lincoln County area. To date, more than 200 accounts have been opened under the program.

-30-

meet with bank officers on Monday nights. Although the teller line was closed, bank officers could take loan applications, work out problems, and open new accounts.

Walker, as bank president, also participated in the Monday program. Each Monday evening, from 7 to 9, both Walker and his senior staff were available to any bank customer—first-come, first-served.

One idea that Walker used arose when an ornate old teller's window was found in a branch basement. Rather than throw it out, Walker instead built a special teller cage with the old window, a teller's cage that was a foot lower than any other in the bank. That cage was designated the children's window and used whenever children were in the branch to open accounts or make deposits. Toward the end of December, when children's accounts were particularly active, the cage was run by a teller in a Santa suit.

Another Walker idea concerned what might be called "platform" marketing. In basic terms, Walker provided the platform and other players received the glory.

For example, on Friday nights when the bank stayed open late Walker made certain that the ornate main branch was filled with music. A grand piano was placed in the bank's huge main lobby and a local high school student—dressed in formal attire—played classical music from 4 to 6. The student was paid for the performance, an account was opened to hold the money, and each player was well publicized with an announcement in the local papers, in school papers when possible, and with cards to friends and relatives announcing the performance.

Another platform program evolved with local merchants. Fashion shows were held at noon on Mondays with local retailers supplying the models and the clothes. Retailers liked the exposure and the chance to show off their inventory. The fashion shows, of course, were well publicized in the local papers.

Professionals were also offered a platform by the bank. Seminars without charge were offered to the public on such topics as tax planning, gardening and how to start a small business with such experts, respectively, as a local CPA, nursery owner, and a speaker from the Small Business Administration. Such programs received good notices in the local papers and often lead to appearances on radio talk shows. The bank not only made professionals happy by providing free space and publicity, it also interspersed outside speakers with its own experts who presented programs on such topics as estate planning and how to get a loan.

Perhaps the most interesting platform programs were the health screenings organized by Fifth National. With a health screening, doctors, nurses, dentists, optometrists and other professionals conduct brief, basic tests to spot problems and determine if further examinations are necessary. A simple blood pressure check, for example, can often show an irregular heartbeat and perhaps the reason why someone experiences fainting spells. An eye examination can often spot diabetes long before other symptoms appear.

Health screenings held in the bank's lobbies not only helped people who needed such services, they also introduced health professionals to potential patients—a benefit appreciated by those who donated services. The bank also benefited: Not only were the screenings regularly covered in the local papers and announced on radio and television, they also brought two sets of accounts to the bank—accounts from those being screened and accounts from the professionals who provided services.

Fifth National, like all banks, was required to make an affirmative effort to extend its operations under the Community Reinvestment Act (CRA). Fifth National wanted to reach all areas of Lincoln County and regarded CRA legislation as an opportunity to devise innovative programs.

Under CRA, Fifth National established four programs to encourage the use of its services throughout the county.

First, the bank established a "Senior Teller Program." Retirees who wished to work as part-time tellers were trained by the bank and then assigned to specific branches near their homes. The attraction of this arrangement was that the bank found a large pool of employees with good interpersonal skills and a lifetime of training.

Second, Fifth National created a "Bank Career Training Program" for local high school students. Under this program Fifth National supplied speakers for career-day programs and established a high-school internship plan. One student was selected from each area high school and allowed to work eight hours per week with the bank. The work was largely clerical but gave students a chance to learn something about banking.

A third program combined community organizations with bank resources. The bank provided free checking for all community-based, non-profit organizations and once each quarter offered a seminar for community group leaders. Typical subjects included bookkeeping requirements for non-profit organizations and information on how to apply for local grants. Community leaders were also invited to the Wednesday breakfast group.

The bank's fourth program was dubbed "Project Access." The bank made certain that all of its branches were accessible to those who used wheelchairs. It installed a TDD for the hearing-impaired and placed braille labels on its automatic teller machines so the equipment would be accessible to the blind.

Under Project Access the bank did something else as well. It provided low-cost loans for businesses and individuals to build ramps and remodel businesses and homes throughout the county. In effect, Project Access not only opened up the bank to those with special needs, it was also a seeding program that could be used throughout the county.

As much as Walker and the bank were interested in Project Access, they were troubled by a basic problem: Handicapped spaces in shopping areas were generally empty, in part because the cost of buying and converting vehicles for use by the handicapped was expensive.

Walker called a local auto dealer and they came up with a joint program: All community agencies that served the handicapped would be polled every six months to find individuals who needed specialized vehicles. The orders would be combined, modifications would be made at cost, low-cost financing would be available from the bank and vehicles would be purchased at fleet rates.

From the dealer's perspective the program made sense because it brought additional sales through the front door, more sales meant a better deal with the manufacturer, and a better deal with the manufacturer translated into higher profits per vehicle.

Fifth National closed many loans under the program and while such financing did not directly maximize profits, it did bring additional business to the bank. Community groups concerned with special needs kept their accounts with the bank. Individuals with handicaps who participated in the program—along with their families, businesses and friends—opened accounts with the bank. And the bank now had a program that required it to regularly stay in contact with dozens of community groups to update order lists and to track the program.

Perhaps most important, around the county handicapped spaces became increasingly filled. People who needed specialized transportation found greater access to the vehicles they needed. Those vehicles, in turn, meant easier commuting and more convenience.

Evaluation

The programs established by the bank to meet CRA requirements produced extensive media coverage. The seminars were often attended by local reporters and the bank's programs to assist high school students, retirees and community groups were frequently covered. The car-buying program generated enormous interest and because the program was ongoing so too was the coverage.

Not to be ignored was another benefit of the bank's well-publicized CRA effort. Because the bank maintained a strong and innovative CRA program, it was able to obtain deposits from government agencies that were set aside for lenders with outstanding CRA records.

As for its huge competitor, it seems that large-scale currency trading produced a single-day loss of $380 million, enough so that Worldwide was forced to lay off 1,800 people and close 120 smaller branches—including those unprofitable outposts in Lincoln County.

TREVOR INSURANCE

Dwight and Alan Trevor work in the insurance business started by their father, Lyle Trevor. Their problem is that to buy out their father's interest in the company they need to generate a larger income stream. They can increase income by finding more clients, providing larger policies, or both.

To make matters more complex, the insurance business is changing. Consumers are looking at larger deductibles to hold down policy costs, more are seeking term life insurance rather than cash value policies, and some large companies offer agentless policies that eliminate a layer of costs and allow for lower pricing.

Advertising in the insurance industry has traditionally been image-based, with such symbols as strong hands, mighty rocks, and comfy blankets. Since the Trevors do not have enough money to launch an image-based campaign, they instead turn to media marketing.

Find the Media

The Trevors visit the library and quickly produce a media contact list. Since they live in a large city, they don't bother with suburban newspapers, but they do find two daily papers, six television stations, 31 radio stations, one city magazine, a weekly business paper and an in-town free advertiser distributed in their neighborhood. Their contact list includes 62 names.

Develop a Program

The tradition with insurance brokers has been to mail renewal notices on an annualized basis, a tradition the Trevors decided to change. Rather than a simple renewal notice the Trevors prepared a personalized, individually typed letter to each client and mailed it about six weeks before renewal notices were scheduled. The letter went like this:

Dear Mr. Smith:

Each year we conduct a special insurance audit for every client without charge or obligation. Please complete the attached form and we will then prepare a computerized statement showing what policies you have, the type of coverage provided and your annual cost. Where possible we will suggest where coverage can be changed to produce lower costs without meaningful reductions in coverage. The audit statement we send back should be included with your insurance records while a second copy is retained in your safe deposit box.

Please complete and return the audit form in the enclosed stamped, self-addressed envelope. Your information will be returned within seven days of receipt.

Sincerely,

Dwight Trevor

Once the form was received the Trevors completed the audit form and then enclosed it within a report folder stocked with several specialized modules.

Working from a client's information, the Trevors might include modules on health, auto and life insurance. Each module would explain how individual policies worked, what they covered, what was excluded, and how the policy could be changed with endorsements. For example, a homeowner's policy can be changed to include full replacement value rather than just a property's fair market value, which might be substantially less.

Through their insurance audit the Trevors obtained four benefits:

- They effectively updated their mailing list.
- They offered a service of value to clients.
- They developed a solid information base.
- They could show clients where coverage was weak or where policies were needlessly expensive.

The last "benefit" might not seem too good for the Trevors, since their business goal was to sell as much insurance as possible. However, the best way to market their product was not to extract a client's last dollar. Instead it was better to give the client a better deal and build client loyalty that would carry over many years.

Another concept developed by the Trevors was a community insurance screening.

Mr. Bill Collins
Metro Editor
The Daily Insight
2120 8th Street
Thornbeck, NJ 02981

Dear Mr. Collins:

Although Thornbeck is usually seen as a middle-class sub-urban community, we have many local residents who qualify for a variety of special insurance programs because of age, income or family size.

The problem is that the very people who are most likely to benefit from such programs are also the people least likely to know about them. We believe many readers would benefit if they were aware of such programs as now exist, and toward that end we are prepared to provide you with a chart we've developed showing six major programs, who qualifies, who to contact and appropriate addresses and phone numbers.

For your records please note that we often make presentations on specialized insurance programs to community groups. We know from the questions asked that many people are simply unaware of the many benefits to which they are entitled.

We hope this letter will be of interest and we look forward to speaking with you at your convenience.

Sincerely,

Alan Trevor

Doctors often provide basic health screenings for selected groups at little or no charge. Such screenings are often able to detect significant problems that can be treated before major problems arise, such as an erratic heartbeat or a need for new glasses.

With an insurance screening the Trevors would speak with members of a particular group, listen to their needs, and then suggest what programs might help them. For example, armed with the proper information and the right forms, someone might qualify for a special program offered through Social Security.

Insurance screenings proved attractive not only because they have value to the individuals counseled, but also because screenings relate to an ongoing media issue—insurance for the poor, the unemployed, and those without adequate Medigap coverage. To make certain it was an issue, the Trevors wrote individual letters to selected reporters inviting them to attend screenings and to speak with community leaders, physicians and hospitals. They soon received coverage in the papers and invitations to appear on radio talk shows, all of which brought business to their door.

Another issue that brought them business was simple English. Half seriously, and half in jest, they developed a seminar entitled "Trevors Irreverent Guide to Insurance: Help for the Disconcerted, the Discomforted and the Perplexed." Filled with usable information, the seminar worked well with community groups, clubs and professional societies.

Obtaining seminar dates was a fairly simple matter since there was no charge to sponsoring organizations. The Trevors made a list of groups they wanted to reach and then wrote to the organization's leader:

Dear Leader:

As you look ahead to the coming year you have undoubtedly scheduled a series of program dates for your members. Among the topics few groups now consider is insurance, a subject which is complex, difficult and rarely of immediate interest.

But what may interest your members is that it is possible to reduce insurance bills today. It is possible to get more and better coverage by just knowing the right questions to ask. It is possible to get substantial tax benefits with the right insurance policies.

Whether you want a two-hour seminar or a luncheon program, we can supply a knowledgeable, noncommercial presentation that will be both entertaining and useful to your members.

As you may know from our many media appearances, we have been able to translate complicated insurance jargon into basic terms anyone can understand. Our presentation is fun, informative and consumer-friendly, and the question-and-answer sessions that follow are always lively.

Just call to schedule a date. There's no charge for our presentation, and since you're local, no expense for transportation or meals.

All the best.

Sincerely,
Alan Trevor

The Trevors used their seminar presentations to establish their name within the local community. Whenever they spoke they brought business cards for those who invariably came up to the platform after their remarks, but they made a point of never bringing sales literature. They also made a point of writing a warm thank-you note after each engagement. Over time they found that they could give two to three presentations a month, each ultimately resulting in one or two new clients.

In many communities real estate brokers also act as insurance agents, often specializing (not surprisingly) in homeowner's coverage. Not all real estate brokers sell insurance, however, and the Trevors were able to identify many who did not.

The Trevors discovered that many real estate firms schedule regular Tuesday morning sessions that often include an outside speaker such as a mortgage loan officer. By contacting various brokers or managers, the Trevors were able to make group presentations at various real estate offices, often using much of the same material that was included in their general seminar program.

Evaluation

The Trevors originally wanted to generate enough new business to buy out their retiring father, but ultimately their media marketing program developed a somewhat different result. A surplus of business and a shortage of time meant they needed experienced help. Their Dad, coaxed out of retirement on a part-time basis, filled their need perfectly.

LANDOVER MORTGAGE BROKERS ASSOCIATION

Mortgage bankers take money from major investors such as insurance companies, and then use it to make loans for local home buyers. In addition to finding funds to finance and refinance real estate, mortgage bankers also "service" loans by collecting monthly payments, remitting funds to investors and foreclosing if required.

The Landover Mortgage Bankers Association is an organization with 50 local members. Although mortgage bankers can include savings and loan associations and the mortgage departments of large real estate companies, in this association only independent firms are members. Thus the lines are drawn: Independent mortgage lenders versus the S&Ls and big realty companies.

What Are the Problems?

Five major problems are outlined in discussions with association officers and directors:

First, national competitors have entered the local marketplace and siphoned off business. These companies have received extensive publicity because they're new, large and have full-time information staffs to attract local coverage.

Second, a computerized "do-it-yourself" mortgage center opened by a local S&L has gotten continuing print and broadcast coverage. Prospective borrowers go downtown, sit at a computer terminal and answer questions posed by a sophisticated computer program. The computer system has attracted borrowers who might otherwise use the services of association members.

Third, a survey conducted by a local college professor, Dr. Numbers, shows 58.6 percent of all prospective home buyers think first of savings and loan associations when looking for a mortgage. Since obtaining a mortgage is a big-ticket, one-time event, being second means not getting business.

Fourth, the Numbers survey also shows 92 percent of all home buyers regard real estate brokers as the major source of financing information. This is a problem because three of the largest real estate companies in town have started their own mortgage origination departments.

Fifth, association members are concerned that a media marketing program structured by the organization may favor one member over another. Instead, everyone wants a program that emphasizes (or creates) a difference between association members and outside competitors.

If the public knew more about association members and their work, the problems seen previously would be less severe. A program is needed that ties mortgage bankers to home ownership in the public's eyes, a program entitled: "Mortgage Banking and You: Partners in Home Ownership."

Find the Media

Association members pool contact lists and find that they can find as many as 215 media contacts in the area they serve. The most important contacts include the real estate editor and writers associated with the downtown daily paper and several radio talk-show hosts who have impressive followings.

Create an Update

To generate ongoing media coverage, the association begins to publish a weekly "Lender's Update" listing the names and phone numbers of each member along with rates for 30-year, 15-year and adjustable rate mortgages (ARMs). Since the listing is competitively neutral, the local daily runs it verbatim in the Sunday real estate section while several publications run the lowest rates in each loan category. Since the survey only includes information from association members, banks, savings and loan associations and non-members are left out.

A Basic Brochure

Public perception is the major problem faced by the association. The general public is largely unaware of mortgage bankers and their role in the financing process. To increase public awareness, the association publishes a basic brochure that describes the mortgage banking system and the general services offered by members.

The association seeks bids on the brochure from ad agencies, graphic artists and writers. In this particular situation, it selects a writer familiar with the business, rather than the lowest bidder, to develop wording. A graphic designer is chosen to lay out the brochure and work with a printer. Seventy-five thousand copies are requested by association members. Adding 10,000 copies for its own use, the association computes the cost of writing, designing and printing 85,000 copies, divides by 75,000 (not 85,000), and charges members according to the number of copies ordered. Using this strategy, the association acquires 10,000 professionally written and designed brochures without cost to itself while providing a standardized document for its members.

Membership Directory

The association has always maintained an informal list of members but a more formal document is required. A printed list is distributed to area reporters and to the public during promotional events.

Experts' Roster

Although a general membership list is valuable, it does not pinpoint members with specialized experience or knowledge, nor does a membership list suggest possible story ideas to reporters. The association creates an "Experts' Roster" for distribution to the media to resolve these problems.

The education committee polls the membership and finds interest in 22 subjects including such topics as "How To Get Your First Mortgage," "How To Buy at Foreclosure," "How

To Speed Your Mortgage," and "What Really Happens at Settlement." Two lists are then established: A subject list showing topics alphabetically while a member list shows names alphabetically and each individual's areas of expertise.

Quarterly Story Concepts

To induce additional media coverage, the association forms a committee to devise ten story ideas every three months. The concepts might be localized versions of national stories or ideas unique to Landover. The story lists are then distributed to area reporters along with the experts' roster.

To give some flair to the project, the quarterly lists are printed on green paper and became known as the "Green Sheets." Among the topics on the first listing are "New Employment Opportunities in Landover Mortgage Industry," "How Washington Mortgage Rules Affect Landover" and "Landover Mortgage Rates Lower Than Other State Areas." The lists are useful to the media and, coupled with the experts' roster, often produce stories quoting association members.

A Local Speakers' Bureau

Landover and its surrounding suburbs are home to hundreds of civic, social and business groups. The association establishes a speakers' bureau and then contacts as many organizations as possible.

The association uses the experts' roster to find speakers and topics. Three hundred target organizations are identified from telephone listings and member contacts and a promotional letter is then sent to each. In addition, a news release announcing the formation of the speakers' bureau is sent to all media contacts.

When a speaking engagement is confirmed, the association names both a speaker and a backup. It's understood that whoever speaks represents the association rather than a particular company under this program. Although no promotional materials from individual firms can be distributed, copies of the basic association brochure and membership list are supplied whenever a member speaks.

A Mortgage Information Hot Line

There is an ongoing demand for home financing information and to meet that demand the association establishes a "Mortgage Information Hot Line." Such a service allows the public to call the association and ask general financing questions in private.

To establish the hot line, the association merely opens its offices from 7 to 9 P.M. on Tuesday and Thursday evenings. Hot-line duty is rotated among officers and members. News releases are sent to the media announcing the new service and fliers developed by the association are given out from member offices. Once the project is established and calls begin coming in on a regular basis, reporters are invited to monitor the service. Several good stories promoting the hot line, and members of the association, result.

Free copies of the membership list and weekly mortgage survey are offered to callers and a follow-up survey shows that a large percentage of hot line users ultimately contact member firms for financing. Just as important, the survey confirms that many callers would not have contacted member firms without the list provided through the hot line service.

A Radio Call-in Program

Although the telephone hot line is a valuable public service, and while it does produce public contact and media coverage for the association, it's necessarily limited to individual conversations that benefit a small number of people. The same conversations can be held on radio to attract a wider audience.

Program directors at all local radio stations are contacted to suggest the call-in program. One all-talk station accepts and the show is set for a 2-to-4 P.M. slot every Friday. A news release regarding the new program is sent to the media and each member distributes fliers to consumers.

The program is set up so that the association president serves as moderator and one or two members answer questions each week. Only members who work on the telephone hot line are eligible to "guest" on the radio program, a policy that produces a large number of hot line volunteers. The basic brochure, membership list and weekly rate sheet are mentioned and sent to anyone calling the station. As an added feature, local journalists are invited on the program to discuss current issues and answer questions from the public.

Help Those with Special Needs

Although the telephone hot line and radio program have the capacity to reach a wide audience, the hearing-impaired are excluded. To broaden its marketplace, the association installs a TDD (Telecommunications Device for the Deaf) phone line in its offices. The TDD line is staffed during office hours and when the Hot Line is open. In addition, it is available to any member wanting to contact individuals with TDD service.

The association contacts civic organizations serving the hearing-impaired for advice on establishing a TDD service. With much encouragement and support from these organizations, the service is established and a release is sent to the general media as well as groups serving the hearing-impaired. In this way community organizations not only help establish the line, but tell members about the new service as well.

In addition, the association surveys member locations to see which ones are accessible to wheelchair users. The list is distributed to media contacts plus a variety of community groups.

What the association discovers is that its programs not only benefit people with special needs, but that such individuals have friends and relatives who also use mortgage banking services. The program generates substantial interest in the association from community segments underserved in the past.

Organize Media Breakfasts

The association and its members usually meet reporters on a business basis, often one that's formal and harried. To create an environment where issues can be discussed in a calm environment and where reporters and mortgage bankers can get to know one another better, the association establishes a weekend breakfast program.

Two or three reporters from different media outlets are invited each week along with the association's executive director, an officer and several members. The breakfasts are held in a downtown hotel between 8 and 9:30 A.M. with 45 minutes given over to eating and the remaining time to current events. The breakfasts become popular with the media because they often produce story ideas and don't interfere with deadlines.

Allied Businesses Programs

Mortgage bankers depend on real estate agents and brokers for referrals and so courting the real estate community is important. The association establishes a formal series of contacts with the real estate community to enhance its referral base.

The association checks with local real estate groups and discovers that to maintain their licenses, real estate brokers and agents must take 15 clock hours of approved continuing education classes each year. The association asks local realty groups to suggest topics that might interest members, forms a committee to develop course outlines and then gets the courses approved by the state. The seminars, jointly sponsored with local realty organizations, are always packed because attendance helps fulfill licensure requirements. The basic brochure, weekly rate summary and membership list are distributed whenever association members lecture. Speakers are drawn from the association's education committee and individuals listed on the experts' roster.

Membership Development

The goal of most organizations is to expand membership. More members means more dollars to support the group's goals and more people to carry out its functions. However, since the members of the association compete not only with non-members but also among themselves for a limited volume of business, and since the association already has enough members to carry out its functions, no effort is made to dilute benefits by expanding the membership. Conversely, membership should not be denied to any interested party that meets the standards established for all current members.

Create a Consumer Library

Although local libraries have extensive personal finance and real estate collections, the association establishes its own mortgage lending library with books, magazines and industry reports solicited from members. A news release notes that the library is available on an appointment-only basis to journalists and the public. Although not used frequently, the library does receive notice in several area publications, and reporters sometimes use the library to research a story.

Premiums

Premiums are often offered to prospective clients in many fields as an inducement to obtain their time, attention and business. Rather than produce its own consumer-oriented handbook, the association contacts several publishers and finds one who offers "How To Save Money When Financing Your Home." In exchange for a bulk sale of 5,000 copies, the association receives a steep discount as well as a customized edition that features the association's name, address, phone number and current membership list.

Once the copies are purchased, a release announcing the availability of the free book through member firms is sent to all media contacts. Over a period of several weeks, nearly all the copies are distributed to consumers, which means almost 5,000 people have direct contact with member firms.

An Outside Speaker

The association decides to produce a consumer-oriented, educational seminar program for the general public. To give the program credibility—and to limit competitive problems inside the association—it is decided to feature an outside speaker.

Speaker Criteria. The oratorical skills of a William Jennings Bryan are not necessary for a seminar program, though such qualities are surely desirable. Instead, the speaker must be a credible individual, someone recognized as an authority figure in the field. Such an individual could be a local mortgage banker, at least in theory, but in practice a local person is unlikely to work because he or she is local and therefore not especially unique to the media; and a local person competes with other association members. What is needed, then, is someone from out of town.

What is also needed is someone with good communication skills, an individual who represents a good story to the media and who knows how to work with reporters.

Given the association's requirement it is agreed that a suitable speaker might include a journalist, author or professor. The speaker should be expected to arrive early, to be available for media interviews, and—if possible—to be a guest on the association's radio program. If an in-studio program with the speaker is not possible, then a phone-feed can be set up.

The association will have someone meet the speaker at the airport and will provide a car and driver so the speaker can readily go to meet with reporters.

Title. The program must be current without being overly specific. "Home Finance Today—How To Cut the Cost of Real Estate Mortgages in Half" is the title created for the program.

The speaker will explain how the mortgage market works, how strong loan applications can be developed and how borrowers can save tens of thousands of dollars, if not more, through such strategies as careful mortgage selection, the use of prepayments, curtailments, refinancing, external savings accounts and short-term financing.

Location. The program will be held in a setting with sufficient transportation, parking and public facilities to assure participant comfort and safety, including access for the handicapped. In considering alternative locations, the association ultimately chooses a downtown hotel for its presentation.

Sponsors.   Association members will be identified as "sponsors" and each will receive a specified number of seminar tickets as well as recognition in the seminar program guide.

Tickets.   Admission will be by ticket only and tickets will be distributed in several ways:

First, association members can log consumer contacts several weeks prior to the seminar and then call each contact ten days before the program to see who wants to attend. This process not only gives members a non-selling reason to call possible borrowers, but also identifies prospects no longer looking for loans.

Second, tickets can be given to regular clients, those frequently in the market for financing.

Third, tickets can be given to real estate brokers and agents, traditionally the industry's largest referral source. Brokers and agents, in turn, can pass the tickets to prospective purchasers (and, hopefully, eventual borrowers).

In each case the offer of tickets to an educational presentation creates opportunities to demonstrate goodwill and enhance credibility.

Timing.   The program is best given on a weekday evening, from 7:30 to 9:30 and divided into two sections with a brief break at midpoint, as follows:

7:00–7:29 Registration
7:30–7:39 Introduction by association officer
7:40–8:29 Speaker
8:30–8:40 Break
8:41–9:00 Speaker
9:01–9:10 Association officer presents local trends
9:11–9:29 Questions and answers
9:30–Close by association officer

Note that although the program is scheduled to end at 9:30, the question-and-answer period may continue until 9:45 or

10 P.M. or possibly later, a factor that should be considered when renting space.

Promotion. Efforts to promote the program should begin four to six weeks prior to the event. Promotion should include the distribution of a cover letter, news release, program outline and speaker biography to media contacts, civic groups and local real estate organizations.

Advertising. The association should establish an advertising campaign noting when tickets will be available from member sponsors, possibly one or two ads in local realty sections. The promotional purpose of such ads is to place the association before the public and help ensure the broad distribution of tickets.

Handouts. Only institutional handouts, such as the basic association brochure, membership roster and weekly rate report should be distributed at the seminar. Materials from individual firms and on-site solicitations will be forbidden.

Public Participation. A sense of participation can be created by allowing audience members to ask questions. A card for written questions can be placed on each seat and then passed up at intermission or to staffers working the aisles during the program. The questions, in turn, can be read from the podium by an association officer. This process creates the aura of participation, gives variety to the program and, not incidentally, allows the association to avoid loud or ego-centered questioners.

Staffing. The association should handle all ticket requests, have personnel available for registration at the seminar, pick up questions from the audience and do such promotional calling and mailing as may be required. In addition, association officers will introduce the guest, speak on local rates, summarize loan preferences and trends, read questions from the audience and close the program.

Budgeting. In evaluating a budget it must be recognized that the total cost will be divided by the membership and that the association itself will incur only minor, out-of-pocket costs. If, for example, there are 50 member/sponsors the cost to participate will be only $226 per sponsor within the projected budget below, hardly an extravagant expense when one considers what the average mortgage banker spends yearly for advertising and media relations.

Alternatively, sponsorship fees can be set above actual costs to compensate the association for organizing and promoting the program. A sponsorship fee of $250 or $300 is reasonable.

A projected budget might include the following costs:

Speaking fee	$5,000
Hotel and transportation	600
Site rental	750
Advertising	2,000
Printing	200
Reception	2,500
Staff overtime	100
Stamps, telephone, etc.	150
Total	$11,300

As an alternative to a flat fee, the association might instead charge members for tickets. If 1,250 seats are available, then each ticket can be priced at $9.05 and offered to members on a first-come first-served basis.

Scheduling. If the first program is a success, then the association should establish a regular seminar program with perhaps one session in the spring and another in the fall.

Evaluation

The association creates a media marketing committee to oversee its projects, polls members every six months to get their reactions to the program, solicits ideas for new projects and files news articles about the association and its members in the library. The local professor, Dr. Numbers, is hired to produce an annual consumer attitude survey.

Over time the association's members increase their share of the market. They become better known to the public and the concept of mortgage banking becomes less murky. Reporters call more frequently than in the past and subsequently there are more stories about association members. The outreach seminars to real estate groups prove successful and the general demand for speakers grows. The radio program and weekly rate sheets give the group ongoing media coverage while the semi-annual speaker's program and occasional premiums attract interest at times that might otherwise be slack.

Index